Trailblazer:
The Extraordinary Life of Diving Pioneer
Dottie Frazier

Edited by Karen Straus • Designed by Bonnie Toth

Through Dottie's generosity and support, proceeds from the sale of this book will be donated to the Women Divers Hall of Fame Scholarship and Training Grant Program.

FIRST EDITION, AUGUST 2019

Copyright ©2019 by Frazier Publications

All rights reserved. No part of this publication may be reproduced, stored in a retrieval system, used on the Internet, or transmitted in any form by any means, electronic, photocopied, or otherwise, without prior permission from the publisher.

Published in the United States by Frazier Publications.
Long Beach, California

Library of Congress Control Number:2019910972

Frazier, Dottie, 1922, July 16 -
Trailblazer: The Extraordinary Life of Diving Pioneer Dottie Frazier
by Karen Straus & Bonnie Toth — 1st U.S. ed.

ISBN: 978-0-578-55198-2

©2019 by Frazier Publications
All rights reserved. First edition 2019.
Printed in the United States of America

Book cover and interior design by Bonnie Toth
Karen Straus, Editor

Disclaimer of Liability
The author, Frazier Publications, and the editor, shall have neither liability nor responsibility to any person or entity with respect to any loss or damage caused or alleged to be caused directly or indirectly by the information contained in this book.

Table of Contents

Foreword
Blazing a Trail 5
    By Bonnie Toth and Karen Straus

In My Own Words 7
    By Dottie Frazier

EARLY LONG BEACH 9
    The Beginning 11
    The Pacific was My Playground 13
    Becoming my Father's 'Son' 15
    Divorce and a Rescue 16
    My Grandparents 17
    Earthquake! 18
    Tent City and The Pike 20
    Scouting 21
    The Y 23
    My Musical Mother 24
    Swims with My Snake 26
    Terry the Tarantula 27
    Milking Rattlesnakes 28
    Snow and Water Skiing 29
    Springboard Diver 30
    School Days 31

BOAT LIFE 33
    The Serenity of Sailing 35
    Birthday Boat 36
    Life Aboard a Cruiser 37
    My First Boat Jobs 38
    'One of the Boys' on a Fishing Boat 39
    Storm at Sea 42

CATALINA ISLAND 45
    The Magic of Catalina Island 47
    Close Call in a Cave 48
    Island Meals 49
    Hunting Abalone 50
    Shark Rodeo 51
    Exploring Wrecks 51

SKIN DIVING 53
    My First Dive 54
    From Look Box to Double Arbalete 55
    Diving for Coins 56
    Diving Derbies 57
    Look Before You Leap 58
    Robbed by a Seal 59

MARRIAGE AND KIDS 61
    The War Years 63
    Building a New Life 64
    A Second Marriage 64
    Family Diving 65

LIFE WITH CYRIL 69
    Looking for Surf and Finding a Husband 70
    Our Days in San Blas 73
    Dredging for Gold 75
    My Love Affair with Harleys 77

THE SCUBA YEARS 79
    Scuba Training 81
    D. Frazier, Scuba Instructor 82
    Nitrogen Narcosis 85
    My Big Lobster 87
    Aboard the *Sea Chase* 89
    Face to Face with a Great White 90

Photo Galleries 93-99

Dottie Stories 101
    A Feisty Gal 103
        By Keith Chase

    Happiness is a Coatimundi 104
    By Cyril May

    Adventure is Her Middle Name 106
    By Eric Hanauer

    Diving with Dottie 109
    By Barbara Allen

    My Firecracker Grandmother 111
    By Jenna Frazier

Sidebars
    Early Long Beach Timeline 10
    Compiled by Dottie Frazier

    Water Sprite 32

    Dottie's Firsts, Honors and Achievements 84

    Training and Accomplishments 92
    Compiled by Dottie Frazier

Acknowledgements 112

FORWARD

Blazing a Trail

By Bonnie Toth and Karen Straus

Dorothy Adell Reider Gath Frazier May. Her name is longer and weighs more than she does, standing barely five feet tall and 100 pounds dripping wet. And dripping with water is how Dorothy Adell has spent much of her remarkably adventurous and long life.

She is better known as simply Dottie, and is a spry, petite and sharp 97 at the time of this writing.

What is amazing about Dottie is not just WHAT she did, but WHEN she did it: Ocean swimming and boating as a child in the 1920s, as well as surfing, skin diving and spearfishing. In the 30s skin diving instructor and commercial fisher in the 40s. Scuba instructor in the 50s and dive shop owner.

And she was still going strong into the 2000s, competing in the 2012 Senior Olympics in billiards, earning four gold medals. She also earned four gold medals in racquetball tournaments. As of 2019 she still uses her treadmill 45 or more minutes a day and just sold her beloved motorcycle. For future birthdays she looks forward to repeating a zipline flight that she enjoyed on her 95th birthday.

Here are a few more of Dottie's life events, achievements and honors over her life (so far).

1933 A 10-year-old Dottie is an eyewitness survivor of the devastating earthquake that leveled parts of downtown Long Beach, California.

1940 Skin diving instructor with the YMCA

1942 Dottie graduates from the United Aircraft School as an aircraft mechanic and works for Douglas Aircraft as a "Rosie the Riveter."

1950 Charter member, Long Beach Neptunes dive club

1955 Los Angeles County Underwater Instructors Certification Course 4 U.I.C.C., the first certified female instructor

1956 Received hardhat diving gear training

1993 *Who's Who in Scuba Diving*, the Academy of Marine Sciences & Underwater Research

2000 Inducted into the Women Divers Hall of Fame

2009 Inducted into International Legends of Diving

2013 Amazing Women Awards, Lifetime Achievement, *Long Beach Press-Telegram*

2014 Awarded the California Scuba Service Award

2019 Awarded the Historical Diving Society Diving Pioneer Award

For complete listings of honors, accomplishments and skills, see page 84.

Dottie tells her extraordinary life story in the following pages. A memorabilia collector and scrapbooker, her words are accompanied by clippings and snaps from her extensive albums carefully compiled over a lifetime. Dottie's penchant for scrapbooking comes naturally. Her mother, Laura Davis Reider, lovingly compiled a beautiful hand-written baby book for her precocious first-born daughter.

A few words about when Dottie started diving. As author and diving historian Eric Hanauer states in his book, *Diving Pioneers*, the primary reason for going underwater in the early days of diving was to hunt fish and shellfish to put on the dinner table. But now, in the 2000s, our oceans are in trouble. A burgeoning human population, environmental degradation and depleted fish and shellfish stocks mean that our oceans are no longer a bottomless cornucopia of food to feed the world, a characterization that we were taught as children growing up in the 1950s.

As divers, underwater hunting is part of our legacy. So when reading about Dottie's exploits, don't judge her by the environmental realities of the 2000s, just enjoy the tales of her underwater hunting for their own sake. And remember, she started skin diving as a child of six or seven, when there were far fewer people, cleaner waters and more marine life.

Of all her many and varied accomplishments, personal and professional, Dottie sums up what means the most to her:

"I love being a mother and homemaker. These are of the utmost importance to me."

— Dottie Gath Frazier

Dottie's parents, Francis D. and Laura Davis Reider, in Washington, D.C. on their honeymoon, February 1921

In My Own Words

BY DOTTIE FRAZIER

Early Long Beach Timeline

Compiled by Dottie Frazier

1884 Wilmore City is renamed Long Beach after developer William Wilmore sells his rights to the seaside California city

1893 Construction begins on the Pine Avenue Pier

1899 Construction on the San Pedro Breakwater adjacent to Long Beach was started to provide a deep-water port for continued growth of commerce. Over the years additional breakwater and sheltering construction was added. Naval vessels moved in and Long Beach became their home port, giving the city the cachet of being a 'navy town'

1900 The population of Long Beach is 2,000

1902 The first electric tram in the city carries passengers from Los Angeles to Long Beach. Tourists arrive in Long Beach to enjoy beautiful beaches, clear water and exciting waves. The Pine Avenue Pier and an amusement park, The Pike are popular destinations. The Pike is called "the Coney Island of the West." A concrete walkway and four-foot seawall along The Pike is constructed to keep high tides and heavy surf from flooding beachfront properties, which were rapidly being built.

1902-1903 The Pine Avenue Pier is reconstructed as a result of age and storm damage. The Pavilion is built at the end of the pier. It burns two months later and is rebuilt, to be enjoyed by tourist for the next 30 years

1904 W.H. and Mattie Reider build and operate the Long Beach Tent City west of The Pike. The demand increases for tourist lodging, the Reider's Tent City was moved to a specially constructed raised deck pier to do away with the problem of high tides. Deluxe 12- by 12-foot rooms with wood floors and walls and canvas tents. A kerosene burner is provided for cooking and heating. A row of showers and flush toilets are included in the price of $1 per day

1908 The first high-end hotel opens, the Virginia on Ocean Boulevard. The beachfront serves as a runway for the first airplane to land in Long Beach

1910 The population of Long Beach reaches nearly 18,000. The city is dubbed "the fastest-growing city in the United States"

1921 Oil is discovered in Long Beach. Long Beach loses its surfing beaches when breakwater construction diverts waves

1925 The first bathing beauty contest is held in Long Beach. Events such as a rowboat race to Catalina Island and channel swimmers racing to Catalina capture the public's imagination

1922 Dorothy (Dottie) Adell Reider is born in Long Beach

1928 W.D. Reider and his son build the Mariner Apartments and Hotel on the site of the old Tent City. They also built on an adjacent site Mariner Annex with a huge beach bathhouse in the basement. This provides a much-needed service for tourists needed bathing costumes, towels and places to change and store clothing

1929 The Great Depression results in many businesses shutting down in Long Beach

1933 A magnitude 6.3 earthquake topples downtown Long Beach. 102 people are killed and more than 140,000 people are left without shelter. Army field kitchens are set up in parks and vacant lots. The Red Cross and Salvation Army provide tents, blankets and meals to the homeless. The Reider family, including 10-year old Dottie, move aboard their well-stocked 30-foot cabin cruiser for the next 30 days

Early Long Beach

Dottie and "Amoo" Reider (grandmother) at the beach, 1924.

The Beginning

I was born on July 16, 1922, and 10 days later I went home from the hospital. My only sibling, a sister, was born on February 26, 1924. My parents, Francis and Laura Davis Reider, lived in a one-bedroom duplex apartment on a hill across the street from the real estate office owned by my dad and grandfather, W. H. Reider. It was located at 528 West Ocean Boulevard in Long Beach, California, one block from the Pacific Ocean. There were garage rentals on both sides of the street down the hill from the office and the duplex where my family lived.

Soon my dad and granddad built a bathhouse closer to the beach at Golden Avenue, and then the original Long Beach Tent City to house the many tourists attracted to the growing city's waterfront. In later years, dad and granddad built the Mariner Apartments and Hotel and the Mariner Annex. Their burgeoning real estate business kept them very busy.

Every day a freight train passed Ocean Boulevard heading from Terminal Island to Los Angeles. I looked forward to my mother taking me up to the top of the hill to wave at the conductor, who, on my first visit, threw me a small box of peppermint candy. By the time Jeanne Adelaide was two years old she, too, was joining mother and me to meet the freight train and get our little box of peppermints. It was a ritual I would never forget and one I always anticipated with delight.

Dottie, her mother and kitty Cycy, 1925.

In My Own Words • Early Long Beach

Dottie and her mother on their yacht, the Dotadell

Pat Shandley, Dottie and Dot Mansell

The Pacific was My Playground

Jeanne and I were baptized at the first Methodist Church in downtown Long Beach, where we attended services and Sunday school with mom. We couldn't get dad to go very often as he often had busy Sundays. When there was time, he would take me and head for his boat on Saturday. We would spend the weekend sailing, fishing and swimming. I liked this better than Sunday school!

He had been taking me out on his sailboat from the young age of six months old. I hardly ever cried so he knew I loved it. I grew up spending many weekends and holidays on the boat.

Reviewing my early childhood with my grandmother, I learned that mom and I went aboard my dad's pride and joy, a 21-foot sloop, when I was only three months old. Mom also loved to sail. Dad named the sloop *Dotadell*, taken from my name, Dorothy Adell. His love of the sea played a big part in his life. He was very knowledgeable in all aspects of boating, both sail and power, and had owned and operated several of each type in the 20- to 40-foot size range.

I started going out with dad on boats when I was only two years old. The Pacific was my playground. I always had my water wings on both in and out of the water. I managed to fall overboard at least once a day, but dad said I did it on purpose whenever he said, "No, you may not go in the water."

By age three I was swimming without the flotation, jumping off the boat, diving head first and able to climb up the swim ladder without help. I had become the son my dad didn't have; being a girl was almost forgotten for many years.

In My Own Words • Early Long Beach

Becoming my Father's 'Son'

Dad was expecting a boy and instead he got two girls. He then decided that he would take his oldest girl and teach her all the things that he had planned to teach to the son. From age six, dad taught me the fine art of boxing. If I had been the boy he wanted, instead of a girl, it would have been logical to know how to protect myself, but he said that my gender made no difference and that I should learn the same things, for the same reasons. There had been a time or two when I wished that I could put a stop to the boys constantly teasing, pushing, hitting and calling me names.

In the harbor area where we had our boat, no girls walked out on the top of the breakwater to fish, swim and dive in, like the boys did after school. As the boys got older and bigger they became rougher and braver, until one day I fought back and gave a few bloody noses and black eyes using my fists as dad had taught me to do. Afterwards I was looked on as an unusual girl not to be messed with.

Little did I realize then that my father's maritime and boxing training would in one way or another shape the rest of my life.

Dottie and her dad, 1978

In My Own Words • Early Long Beach

Girl of 7 Plunges Into Ocean to Save 5-Year-Old Sister

Dorothy Reider, daughter of Mr. and Mrs. Francis D. Reider, 206 Pomona Avenue, is only 7 years old, but she demonstrated her ability as a swimmer and a life saver recently when she leaped from her parents' yacht, the Mariner, into thirty feet of water just inside the harbor entrance and rescued her 5-year-old sister, Jean, who had fallen overboard.

Mrs. Reider and other members of the family were below, when they heard a splash. On hurrying to the deck they found Dorothy holding her younger sister afloat.

Mr. Reider was sailing a small skiff several hundred yards away and did not know of the near tragedy until after the rescue had been effected.

Divorce and a Rescue

When I was three, family life changed when my parents divorced. Dad was given custody of me with visitation rights for my mother. One-year-old Jeanne went with my mom. I spent the majority of the next few years with dad living on the *Mariner*, a 28-foot yawl, in the harbor of Long Beach, just off Terminal Island. When I was old enough I went to school from the boat to a one-room schoolhouse with only a few kids about my age. On many weekends mother and my sister joined us on the boat.

On one occasion, when my mother was down in the galley fixing lunch and dad was out in the sailing skiff, Jeanne fell overboard with no floats on. I was fishing nearby. I dropped my pole and jumped over the side, grabbing my drowning sister. I was seven years old. I could not reach anything to grab, and I didn't know how long I could tread water. But even with all of her struggling and yelling, I managed to keep Jeanne's head above water. Mother heard our calls for help and came up on deck to find us both in the water. She immediately pulled us to safety.

Dad wasn't aware of the near tragedy until he returned to find mother trying to dry and calm my hysterical baby sister. From that time on Jeanne always wore water wings or floats on when on deck. My sister was not that interested in marine life and didn't come out that often.

From about age six on a permanent home was not to be had for me. However, I had my grandparents, aunts, dad and his girlfriends (there were plenty!), private schools, boarding schools and housekeepers. I never knew who was going to be looking after me next. I guess this is one of the reasons I became so self-reliant early in life.

My Grandparents

When weather prevented dad and me from taking our boat to Catalina Island I spent time with my wonderful grandparents, W.H. and Mattie Reider. I called my grandmother Amoo. I have many happy memories of spending time with them.

After my parents divorced, I spent some time during many summers going on camping trips all over the Western states with my dad and his folks. I learned how to survive in the wilderness, how to freshwater fish, backpack, build safe fires for cooking, and much more, including hunting.

It was while staying with Amoo that I learned as many of my grandma's secrets in cooking that I could because she was the best. She also taught me how to make my own clothes. Grandpa was a wiz at all kinds of fun games and great at helping me with my homework.

When on camping trips with dad is where I learned how to use and care for many different kinds of guns, from revolvers to rifles, how to build fires, how to fix complete meals in ground ovens, using the hot coals to bake a multi-course meal. They were all excellent freshwater fishermen so I was blessed with excellent instructors in this, another field. We climbed mountains, rode the rapids in kayaks, and floated down rivers on inner tubes. Those were times very dear to me and are ones that I will never forget.

My grandparents came from a farm in the Midwest, so Amoo taught me how to make jams and jellies and can all sorts of food. Some distant relatives from Kansas had bought a big farm about 75 miles from Long Beach and we went out to visit them. I learned to ride horses, milk cows, feed pigs, drive farm equipment, skin rabbits, pluck chickens and plant a garden. I loved everything about farm life, but would never trade it for my time on the boat.

Dottie May recalls 1933 earthquake as a big adventure

By Rich Archbold

Dottie May Frazier was only 10 years old when a devastating earthquake hit the Long Beach area on March 10, 1933, but she remembers it like it was yesterday.

"I woke up to find white lilies all over my body and I was very wet," she recalled last week. "Then I remembered that I had been sitting by the fireplace in our living room doing my homework when the room started going up and down and around and I couldn't get up. The large vase above me on the mantle had fallen off and landed on my head and knocked me out."

Frazier didn't know what had happened and screamed for her [mother] but she didn't answer. [...] ladder in bedroom and found my mother and 7-year-old sister on the floor hugging each other and crying. We managed to get outside and joined our neighbors," she said.

Frazier was one of many lucky school children to survive on that fateful day 81 years ago on Monday.

The deadly magnitude-6.4 earthquake struck at 5:54 p.m. on a Friday evening, just hours after Long Beach's 28 schools were filled with children. More than 100 schools in the Long Beach, Compton and Huntington Park areas were severely damaged or destroyed.

Jefferson Junior High in Long Beach was one of those schools. And Jefferson was Dottie May's school.

"My school would not resume until the fall session due to the extensive damage," she said.

Although school children were spared, many others were not so fortunate. More than 120 people were killed, including 53 in Long Beach, making it the state's second deadliest earthquake. Property losses were estimated at $50 million in 1933 dollars.

When she fled from her Belmont Shore house with her mother and sister, Frazier said they were told by police officers and firefighters to move to vacant lots and wait for Army units to arrive.

"It wasn't long until we were being served dinner by soldiers," she said.

"Around 8 we heard a loud-speaker from a police car announcing that there was a dangerous tidewater coming and for all to head for Signal Hill which was the closest high spot.

"Mom and my sister rod the front seat of her 1929 roadster, and I grabbed my cat, Mouchy, and pet rat and got into the rumble seat for the ride. Others who got there before us had a big fire going which had been built out of discarded tires. Early the next morning we were told that the tidal wave was a false alarm and we could go back to our home."

Like many 10-year-olds, Dottie May said she treated the disaster as "a great adventure."

In fact, that's how she's treated her entire 91 years of life, soon to be 92 on July 16.

Although she barely weighs 100 pounds, her lifetime achievements are legendary. She was the world's first female "hard hat" deep sea diver, the first female scuba instructor in the U.S., and a member of the Women Divers Hall of Fame, [...] the Riveter" with Douglas Aircraft, a swimsuit model, a competitive billiards player and a water and snow skier. She knows how to fix auto transmissions, and she still drives her own car. She is an expert gardener.

Her list of accomplishments is so long, she was named a Lifetime Achievement recipient in the Press-Telegram's fourth annual Amazing Women Awards program last year.

But don't think Dottie May is slowing down. She still gets up early in the morning to tend her fruits and vegetables garden and has coffee, peanuts and raisins with friendly squirrels and her favorite bird, "Mr. Blue."

If you're in the neighborhood, she would invite you in, too.

Rich Archbold is public editor of the Press-Telegram. rich.archbold@langnews.com

Dottie May Frazier was 10 years old when the 1933 Long Beach earthquake knocked her unconscious. She lived with her family in Belmont Shore and recalled the windows and doors had to be replaced, but the foundation was intact. She is holding a photo of herself at age 10, in 1933.

PHOTO BY BRITTANY MURRAY — STAFF PHOTOGRAPHER

LOCAL NEWS

HISTORY

One lucky lady

The 1933 earthquake was a scary adventure for longtime Long Beach resident, 95

It's hard to imagine Dottie May Frazier, now a feisty and fearless 95-year-old with a lifetime of legendary achievements behind her, as ever being scared.

But she admitted last week that she was "scared to death" when the 1933 Long Beach earthquake shook her house in Belmont Shore on March 10, 1933.

It's no wonder. Dottie May was only 10 years old and was knocked unconscious by the destructive quake. Although the quake happened 85 years ago, the memory is forever etched in her brain. She remembers it like it was yesterday.

"I remember sitting by the fireplace in my living room doing my homework when the room started going up and down and around, and I couldn't get up," she told me.

"The large vase above me on the mantle had fallen off and landed on my head and knocked me out. I climbed up the ladder in the closet that led to an upstairs bedroom and found my mother and 7-year-old sister on the floor hugging each other and crying. We managed to get outside and joined our neighbors."

Earthquake!

Editor's note: *In the Sunday, March 4, 2018 Long Beach Press-Telegraph, Dottie was featured as an eyewitness survivor of the deadly 6.4 magnitude earthquake that cut a swath across the Newport Beach-Inglewood fault line 85 years earlier, on March 10, 1933. The quake killed 102 people, 53 of them in Long Beach. It struck at 5:54 pm, scant hours after thousands of children had been released from school. More than 100 school buildings in Long Beach, Compton and the Huntington Park areas were severely damaged or destroyed, including the school 10-year-old Dottie attended. One month after the quake the California Legislature passed the Field Act, mandating improved building codes for new schools to resist earthquakes.*

The following is Dottie's eyewitness account.

I woke up on March 10, 1933, to find Calla Lilies all over my body. I was also very wet. I remembered that I had been sitting by the living room fireplace of my mom's house at Belmont Shore, Long Beach. I was doing homework when the room started going up and down and around and then things went black. The large vase on the mantle above me had fallen and hit my head, knocking me out. Only 10 years old at the time, and confused about what was happening, I screamed for my mom. When she didn't answer, I tried to go out the front door but the door would not open. The back door was also jammed. I remember that my mom and sister were upstairs, so I climbed up the ladder in the closet leading to an upstairs bedroom. There I found my mother sitting on the floor comforting my distraught 7-year-old sister. We managed to get outside and join our neighbors.

There were policemen and firefighters telling people to stay out of their homes. We were directed to nearby vacant lots. About 8 pm we heard a loud speaker announcing that a dangerous tidal wave was coming

Trailblazer: The Extraordinary Life of Diving Pioneer Dottie Frazier

and anyone with transportation should head for Signal Hill. Mom and my sister rode in the front seat of her 1929 roadster and I grabbed my cat and pet rat and got into the rumble seat. Being March, it was cold at night. When we arrived, a bonfire of discarded tires had been started and was kept alight through the long night to help people stay warm. I also remember people singing to pass the hours.

Early the next morning we were told that the threat of a tidal wave was a false alarm. We were more than ready to head back to the canteen breakfast line. The army was passing out blankets, cots and water. Later we were informed that all gas, water and electricity was out and that know one knew when it might be restored.

Many buildings were damaged beyond repair, including churches, schools and hospitals. Downtown Long Beach was especially hard-hit. My school, Jefferson Junior High, would not re-open until the fall, if at all.

Three days after the quake we were told that we could go back home. Some doors and windows needed replacing, but the foundation was not damaged. We got our drinking water from the army, used kerosene lanterns for light and still could not cook or bathe. We were dependent on the army for nearly everything.

We were more fortunate than many displaced residents, as my dad had a 30-foot cabin cruiser moored on the harbor. He moved us aboard. The boat was stocked with canned goods, water, a galley for cooking, battery powered lights, linens and first-aid necessities.

Being only 10 at the time of the quake, I was at first very scared. But I soon treated the disaster as a great adventure, as I'm sure other children did. I wrote this story at the age of 92, and my memories are as vivid as if it happened yesterday.

My grandmother, Mattie Reider, wrote the following poem in January, 1934. She tells the story better than I could.

— Dottie

The tenth of March, nineteen thirty-three,
Was a momentous day for you and me.
The end of all things it seemed at the time,
But shielded and guarded by a power divine.
What a different story we can now relate,
Than appeared to be ours on that awful date.

T'was late in the day, almost six o'clock,
When a violent jerk the earth began to rock.
In all directions it seemed to go,
Rocking and swaying to and fro.
Upward and downward, faster and faster,
Bringing upon us death and disaster.
What a pitiful sight we gazed upon,
Homes and churches wrecked, school buildings gone.

Did Long Beach give up? Well let's see,
That was March tenth, thirty-three,
By January fourth, thirty-five,
Our city was very much alive.
Disaster had taught us to pull together,
Homes and churches are better than ever.
Our schools are finished, being safe and fine,
Having strength and beauty in every line.

Rains are bountiful, grass is green,
Flowers are lovelier than we've ever seen.
Tourists arriving every day,
Many who will decide to stay.
Old Man depression is on the run,
The new Long Beach has just begun.
The future looks bright for you and me,
In our beautiful city beside the sea.

Tent City and The Pike

Dad was kept busy managing a dozen canvas and wood tents next to the beach, built up on a pier to keep them from being washed away by the high surf in that area. It was called The Long Beach Tent City. These tents were about 10 feet by 12 feet with up to four army cots (depending on how many people were in the party), four folding chairs, a small table, a two-burner alcohol stove, an ice box, a three-drawer dresser and a folding six-hanger closet. Larger tents were available, if needed.

Tourists reserved them months in advance of the summer season, to be right at the beach. Dad's other business was a bathhouse right across the street and was another big draw of tourists from nearby cities. For $1.00 you were given a large wooden box to put all your clothes in, a wool bathing suit in your size, a locked security box and key for valuables, and directed to a private dressing room. When you were ready to leave, your clothes were stored in a locked room and you received a special waterproof tag that you could secure to the wrist with a number that matched the one on your box to get your clothes out of the storage area.

The beach right out in front was especially popular because of the big surf. We had lifeguards ready to rescue swimmers and inexperienced body surfers who got caught in riptides. I had been surfing there almost before I could walk, and no breaker would be too big for me to catch and ride it all the way into the shallow water. Dad and I were always in competition to see which of us could get the longest ride. It was a sad day when the breakwater was built two miles from the shore to protect the Navy fleet homeported in Long Beach. Unfortunately for us, the breakwater eliminated all surfing activity.

When dad had a night free we would walk down to The Pike, the big amusement center just about a mile east. We would have our favorite meal of chili and beans and a big frosty malted milk. There were so many things to ride in or on that it was difficult to choose. However we both agreed that our favorite ride was the big Jackrabbit roller coaster. That old original name stuck for many years, even after the Cyclone Racer was built to replace it in 1930. I also liked the Hippodrome merry-go-round, where each circle made you would get the chance to grab a ring sticking out on a long tube. If you were lucky to grab the gold ring you would get to ride again free. I was usually lucky and got a lot of rides.

The Pike Plunge was a famous place then. It was a saltwater pool with a big fountain where people could stand with water pouring out the top. The depth varied from two to five feet for children and waders, and a deeper area of 10 to 12 feet for swimmers, as well as springboards and diving platforms at different heights.

Dottie at Tent City, 1937

Scouting

My mother became one of the first commissioners for the Girl Scouts of America in Long Beach, and I was the first girl to join the first troop in Long Beach. I was very active and spent some time selling hot cross buns and Girl Scout cookies with all my friends. Shortly after I became a Girl Scout dad brought home an old bugle. Where he got it I have no idea but anyway I had a lot of fun trying out all the calls that I'd heard played at different locations. I got pretty good at it. I decided to add it to my many accomplishments and decided to take it to the Scout camp when I went.

My goal was to see how many badges and awards I could earn. It took me at least two years to get just about every badge offered in our manual. Most of the girls had never been exposed to many of the badge categories: seamanship, swimming, boating, camping, hunting, taught me. I breezed through those with no trouble, earning more badges than anyone else. I looked forward to going to the official Girl Scout camp in the mountains with other troops from Long Beach.

The scout leaders found out I could blow the bugle and I was put to the task of sounding reveille, taps and a few other calls I had to learn. But I added to my store of knowledge from dad by attending many of the different classes and categories that were offered at camp. He lectured at camp on freshwater boating versus ocean boating, nature study and reptiles. Every summer I spent there allowed two weeks per girl in camp, as long as it didn't interfere with the previously planned family vacation.

Dottie, front row, third from the left, with her Girl Scout troop.

In My Own Words • Early Long Beach

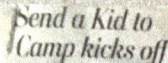

Send a Kid to Camp kicks off

The camp's "oldest kid" Dottie Frazier, 94, poses with 160 camp members last year with a banner in memory of Press-Telegram columnist Tom Hennessy who started the Send-a-Kid-to-Camp Fund with Jean Bixby Smith of the Long Beach Community Foundation. The fund seeks donations each year to send underprivileged children to summer camp for a week.

Dottie's father, Francis Reider, was very involved in starting the YMCA Camp Oakes, and they even have a cabin named for him. Dottie returned for a number of years to break her own record as the oldest person to ride their zip line until she turned 95!

July, 2014

July, 2014, 92 years "young!"

Dottie all dolled up for one of the YMCA dinner events.

July, 2017. Dottie zipping around at the YMCA Camp Oakes in Big Bear, California at age 95!

22   Trailblazer: The Extraordinary Life of Diving Pioneer Dottie Frazier

The Y

Editor's note: *The following text is from a speech Dottie gave, recalling her lifelong involvement at the Greater Long Beach YMCA.*

Good evening, fellow supporters of the Y! I am honored to be here with you tonight and to be able to share a small portion of my story with the Y.

My story begins before I was born with my father's involvement in the YMCA. At age 12 he was one of the first and youngest members of the Long Beach YMCA. He continued his involvement throughout his life and contributed many hours and dollars to help grow the YMCA into what it is today, including building the new pool at the second downtown YMCA, which was built in 1921. Towards the end of his life he received a beautiful award, which I still have in my home today, recognizing his 70 years of service to the YMCA.

As a child I remember wanting to go swimming at the YMCA with my father, but at that time females were not allowed to go to the YMCA. However, my father loved to play handball at the Y and as he didn't have anyone to watch me while he played, I often got to go along. I would play by myself in the court next to his. He would come over after his game and teach me how to play.

One day in 1928, after my father had finished his game, the president of the Y, Robert Gossom, came over to the court where I was playing and told me that for my upcoming sixth birthday they were going to have a special party and surprise just for me. Sure enough, on my birthday there was a party with all of my dad's Y friends. The president brought his son, who was my age, and we all had cake.

During the party Mr. Gossom presented me with my very own membership to the YMCA of Greater Long Beach. I was the first female member of the Long Beach Y. (Membership was not extended to all females until the end of World War II.) I was very surprised and honored to be presented with a membership. But I still couldn't go swimming for several years, since the wool swimsuits of the time would clog the pool filters. *(Editor's note: It was common at the time for males to swim in pools without swimsuits.)*

Another one of my father's important projects with the YMCA was building the staff lodging up at the YMCA Camp Oakes. He hoped that one day his daughter and grandchildren would be able to come to camp and stay in the cabin he helped build.

For my 94th birthday I was finally able to go up and stay for the weekend at Camp Oakes, where I spent time with the children and counselors and stayed in that same cabin built by my father. It meant a lot for me to be able to spend time with the kids at camp and to be able to sit down and have a meal with them.

As an adult, I formed my own connections with the YMCA. I served for 20 years as a volunteer, teaching everything from scuba diving to first aid, canoeing and sailing. I would bring in my own boats and I would encourage new members to the YMCA by getting them to sign up for my classes.

While I have many, many more stories that I would love to share with you from those 20 years, I will leave you with this thought: I truly believe that I was put here to work for the YMCA and that work has been a great blessing in my life, and I hope a blessing to our community.

I encourage you to continue to your support of the YMCA and I hope that you will be blessed as I have been, while blessing those around you through your support of the great work being done every day at YMCA.

If you have the opportunity, I would encourage you all to take time to go and visit the YMCA and YMCA camps. Your support is making a difference for many people.

Mom & me, 1937.

My Musical Mother

I enjoyed the time I had with mom. She was a wonderful piano player and had a beautiful voice. We had lots of music every day I learned to sing harmony with my sister who was only five. We were billed all over town as the Flower Sisters and sang at many churches, special parties, school functions where my mom always accompanied us on the piano. We had many family gatherings on holidays, as well as birthdays and anniversary celebrations. This also gave me the chance to practice lots of cooking and baking. As far as I know no one ever got sick or died.

One evening when I was sitting at the dinner table with dad and my grandparents, dad was explaining to his mom and dad how he had just come from a funeral for an old aunt of theirs. Since he had been appointed the

administrator of her estate it was up to him to oversee having her old home on Terminal Island torn down and the contents donated to the Salvation Army.

The only item of interest was an old violin that her husband used to play. He suggested that I be given music lessons on the violin. A few days later dad brought the violin home.

I had hoped to play the piano like my mother, but she played by ear, a special gift she had since child. She only needed to hear any tune just once and could sit right down at the piano and play it through beautifully. My grandparents, who I lived with at that time, had an old player piano, but not in good enough condition for me to take lessons.

Eventually I became good enough on the violin to play in the school orchestra and also in a violin quartet. But I have to admit that I still didn't like the violin. Little did dad know how many times I did everything I could think of to keep from having to go to my lessons. I would fray the strings so that at least one would break in the middle of the lesson and I would never have a replacement. I even frayed one end of the bow so that it would be impossible to use it during the lesson. My music teacher came to the rescue when she suggested to dad that I should forget the violin for a while and take up another instrument.

My dad was so pleased at my success in learning the violin that he approved my request for taking lessons on my favorite instrument, the accordion. My new instrument went with us on all of our camping trips, where I entertained many of the neighboring campers around our campfire every evening.

On many weekends we also cruised out to the outer harbor on our boat, serenading all of the navy personnel standing at the railings of the various ships: destroyers, battleships, cruisers and other ships in the fleet. Appreciation was duly noted by all of the yelling, clapping, and whistles we got. I also found jobs playing on fancy yachts during trips to Catalina. I was the entertainer while the lunch was being served to passengers. Afterwards I would dive for coins thrown in the water, which also entertained the passengers and got me more pay.

Swims with My Snake

I had always loved snakes and lizards and had a six-foot Gopher Snake named Buddy, who was my best friend for a few years. He rode draped around my neck when I went skating or bicycling.

I was with my grandparents most of the time now, and every morning I got up very early, got Buddy and ran the two blocks to the ocean. There was a 40-foot bluff above the beach and the waves would crest about 100 yards from shore, building up more power as they reached shallower water. Then, with a great crash on the sand, the wave would roll up the bluff 10 or 15 feet and drop back down and out to sea.

With Buddy wrapped around my neck, I would wait for a big wave to roll up the bluff. Then I would dive in and ride the retreating wave out to deep water. When I started my swim paralleling the shore, Buddy would slip off my neck and swim by my side for the usual half mile. Buddy would make the turn with me and swim back to our starting point. He would then wrap around my neck until I caught a good wave and body surfed into the beach and on up the bluff, all without a scratch to either of us.

I guess we put on quite a show. Every morning there were people on the top of the bluff by the railing waiting for my arrival. They always waited until I had completed the swim and was back on shore. Many of the onlookers asked if they could touch Buddy. It was the first time most of them had ever touched a snake.

And, as you can see, Dottie's love of snakes has never gone away.

Terry the Tarantula

I have always been interested in reptiles. Hearing about an exhibit of reptiles being offered down at the Pike, I asked my grandmother if she would take me to see it. She kept putting me off with one excuse or another until one day she said, "I have a surprise for you, we are going to the exhibit on the Pike that you've been wanting to see for a long time."

On camping trips I had collected quite a few different species of lizards and snakes and had them in many different cages stacked on top of each other against the walls in my bedroom at my grandparent's house. I increased my collection quite by accident when my grandma took me to the Pike on Saturday to see the advertised show. We found the booth that we were looking for, thanks to a big sign, "Come in and see the poisonous snakes, giant 20-foot pythons and many other reptiles."

A man came out of the room in back and stood on a podium. There were a lot of people standing around waiting for him to speak. We managed to squeeze through the crowd to the stage, so I could see. He talked for five minutes or so explaining what a ticket to the exhibit would let them see. Then he reached into a box by his side and brought out a big, hairy, long-legged tarantula and placed it on his arm. It was big enough to cover a dinner plate. This spider was only dangerous when alarmed or being attacked. Then it would defensively protect itself.

It was explained to us the tarantula's feet were sensitive to touch, and if pushed could result in a bite. It was then that he noticed the absence of the spider and immediately asked, "Does anyone see where it is?" Some man spoke out and told him it was at the back of his head by his neck. The man seemed to get very nervous, then asked if someone would please come up on the stage and remove it before it might get one of its eight legs caught in his collar, possibly resulting in a bite. No one volunteered.

It was a shock to the crowd to see a little girl walk up on to the stage, climb up on a stool by the presenter, reach up and lift the big spider down and hand it to an amazed, speechless man. People clapped and yelled, my grandma fainted, and I got lots of hugs. I came home with a lifetime pass to the show, a gift of the tarantula (whom I named Terry), his cage, my choice of five snakes with cages and a month's supply of food for all. This was what increased my collection.

As a result of having to feed 20 different species of reptiles, I had to start raising mice and rats, which didn't make grandma very happy. She rarely went into my room and the door was always closed. She did, however, get a kick out of taking lots of her visitors down the hall, cautiously open my bedroom door just a crack, telling them to take a quick peek but not to hold the door open, even a little bit, as there could be something on the loose, trying to find a way to get out of the room.

It would have been much too expensive to buy food for my collection, so I built extra cages in the garage, back yard, and under the second-story stairs. I had a male mouse and a male rat and five females of both species, which gave me more than enough young ones to use for snake food. Some of the smaller reptiles ate all types of insects, frogs, small lizards and pollywogs, which kept me very busy taking care of my big family.

Milking Rattlesnakes

While attending Polytechnic High School in Long Beach I took any biology and natural science classes that were available. I was especially interested in snakes. I had several rattlesnakes in my collection, and had heard of the need for hospitals to have antivenom to treat people bitten by a rattlesnake. The antivenom is made from the venom of rattlesnakes.

It was summertime and reptiles were emerging in large numbers in the hills around Long Beach. I explained to a teacher what I had in mind, and needed his opinion and permission to try and help provide this vital medicine. He gave me his okay, and asked the class if there were any volunteers to go with me on a snake hunt. Five or six boys answered yes; no girls responded. The boys were ready to go if their parents granted permission.

We got together the next Saturday and went to my dad's workshop. He helped us make snake sticks, which we needed to hold the snake tight to the ground. The boys had already learned how to properly hold a harmless snake in class, pinching the head with their thumb and forefinger. We also armed ourselves with several longer sticks with the hook part of a wire clothes hanger. We would use this to reach into rocky areas and pull snakes out before pinning them to the ground. We also brought along several sturdy wooden boxes topped with screen covers. There was a small opening into which the snake could be quickly dropped and the opening closed.

I chose Palos Verde Hills as our hunting grounds, since it was close and had not yet been built up. I figured that the group was well prepared. We wore good boots, had water canteens, sunglasses and packed lunches. I also brought a first-aid kit and a snakebite kit, which I hoped I didn't have to use.

No more than 10 minutes after we had parked the car and set off up a brushy trail through rocks, when I heard a rattle indicating a nearby snake. It was in a coiled position and I forced it to strike, causing it to stretch fully out. This allowed me to put my snake stick right over its head and onto its neck. The boys stayed back and out of the way until I had a good grip on the snake's head. I then picked it up and dropped it into one of the boxes.

In the next couple of hours we found and captured four other good-sized snakes. They were in the boxes and ready for the trip back to school. Our teacher was waiting for us so we could transfer the snakes into special cages in the classroom.

The next step would be to milk the snakes of their venom. During class on Monday I opened a snake cage and with my snake stick holding the snake down tight, got a good grip on the back of the head and both sides of the neck, where the venom sacs are located. I had my small glass ready, its top tightly covered with a piece of netting. By forcing the snake to open its mouthing pressing the fangs down through the netting I could press against the venom sacs, forcing the liquid down into the bottle.

This is how you milk a rattlesnake.

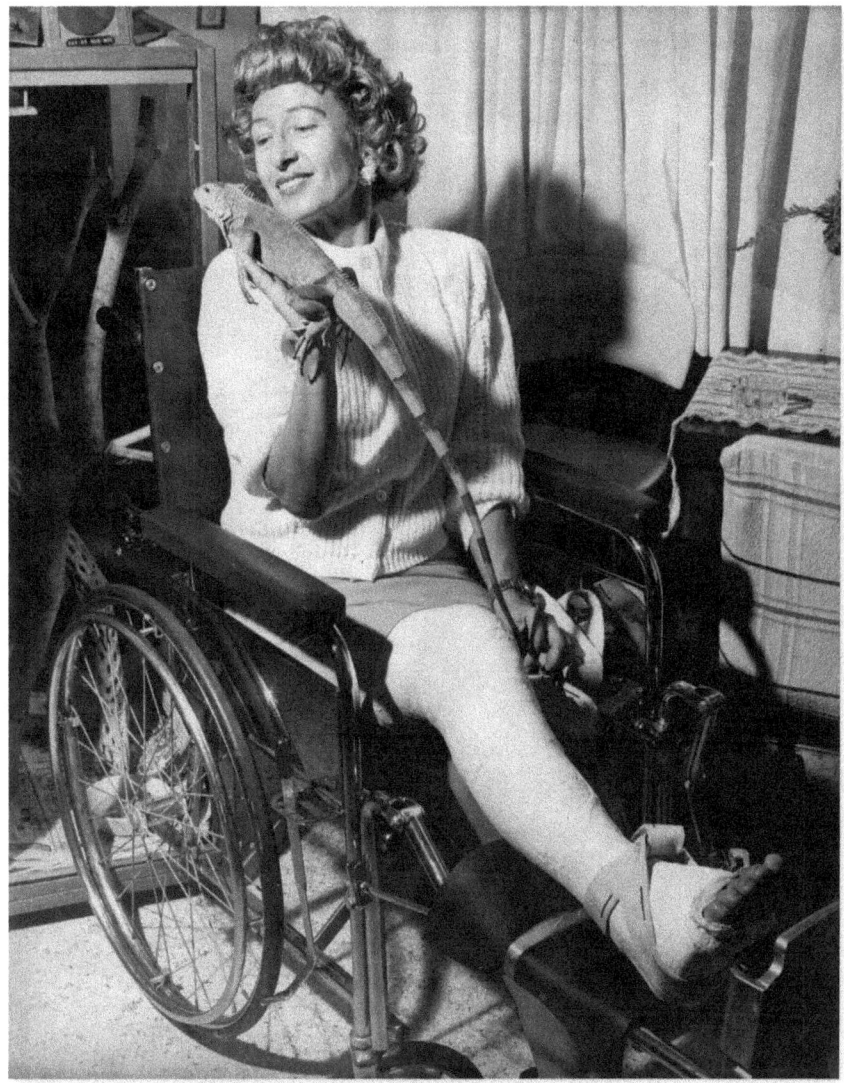

Snow and Water Skiing

My mother had remarried and moved up to Big Bear in the mountains, just a couple of hours' drive away. It was my chance to learn a winter snow sport. I took to snow skiing like a duck takes to water and looked forward to heading for the slopes as often as possible.

Since snow skiing was so seasonal I also started doing a lot of water skiing, which was very popular in the Long Beach area, in both the ocean and in the large bays.

I joined an acrobatic team of water-skiers and we put on numerous shows. There were three boys and three girls. We did jumps, used our legs to hold the towline and performed on single skis. The girls would climb on the shoulders of our partners and do numerous acrobatic tricks, all three teams at the same time. I loved the sport and if and when I fell during practice, it sure didn't hurt as much as when I fell off my snow skis.

Falling off my snow skis resulted in a spiral fracture to one leg and I ended up in a cast for two years. I told the doctor if he didn't take the cast off I would go diving with the cast on. For the last six months of treatment I had a leg brace and a special wetsuit with a full leg zipper. My buddies would remove the brace, zip me into the wetsuit and lift me over the side, handing down equipment to me. I did all my kicking with one leg until the injured leg was completely healed.

I managed to hunt my limit of lobster, despite the handicap!

Springboard Diver

My training as a fancy diver on diving boards and platforms started from the top deck of the boat. I learned how to do a jackknife, swan, back and front flips and somersaults. High diving was one of dad's special talents. In college he won many trophies for diving and was determined to teach me. He took me to a private pool where I became proficient in many different dives from the higher platforms. He had big ideas of getting me in the city Junior Olympics when I reached 10 or 11 in age.

I spent many months in the huge swimming pool at The Pike in downtown Long Beach, perfecting my skills. My only mishap in that time occurred when I was practicing my handstand dives and didn't straighten out early enough and broke my nose on the bottom.

I took advantage of the many high diving platforms at the deep end of the pool. I never tired of watching dad do his many amazing dives. I was now ready for my first real competition for Junior Olympics hopefuls. A short time later the city announced the Junior Olympic diving contest with girls and boys between 10 and 15 years old. He signed me up right away.

As near as I can remember there were 16 boys and girls with the same hopes. It was held at Alamitos Bay in the summer where there were diving platforms of varied heights. After about two hours, and all the contestants had performed about seven different dives, it was announced that I had made the finals, tied with another girl my age. Both of us had to do the swan dive again to break the tie. She went first and made a poor entry. I crossed both

Dottie (mother of two!) 1942

fingers, climbed to my assigned level, took a deep breath and made my dive.

I don't remember anything after that until I regained consciousness in the hospital, strapped to a body board. I was told that I had 13 lineal fractures of my lower back and it was uncertain if I would ever walk again. I was in the hospital many months.

It seems that a man was watching the diving from the platform one level above mine. He evidently thought that after my opponent made her dive that the competition was over. He jumped in feet first, hitting my back just before I hit the water. The force was so powerful that I was pushed under the water and I came up underneath the dock. In the confusion of lifeguards diving all over looking for me, getting the ambulance, doctors, police etc., the culprit responsible disappeared into the crowd and was never seen again. To this day I can't ever remember going a whole day without back pain.

After leaving the hospital a therapist came to my mother's home where I was staying that school term. It was months later, still doing daily exercise that I thought would never end, before I could sit up for short periods without my braces on.

I was soon back skin diving every chance I got. I took up tennis and racquetball when I was sure I was ready and played for many years to come. In later years I won four Gold Medals in the Long Beach Senior Olympics for racquetball.

School Days

The summer before I was to start high school I kept up with all of my sports, anticipating the coming year. While attending Rogers Junior High I had signed up for Wilson High School, but discovered that Wilson didn't have the science courses that I wanted, plus I wasn't living in the correct district. We were informed that living with my grandparents my school district was Polytechnic High School. Polytechnic had a great choice of science classes. Dad was elated; he had graduated from the same school in 1913.

My favorite class was zoology and second, physical education. I learned the new, and getting very popular, game of soccer. I played water polo and joined the surfing and swimming teams. It was a long walk from home each day, but I still continued my early morning swims with my snake. Dad and I still went to Catalina Island whenever he could find the time, where we continued our diving, spearfishing, sailing, aquaplaning and water skiing.

When junior high school let out for the summer I joined the Red Cross and became a certified instructor in small craft, sailing, canoeing, kayaking, water safety, lifeguard, and first aid. I began teaching many classes in various swimming pools and at Alamitos Bay. Skin diving was becoming a very popular sport and I taught more of those classes than any of the others.

Polytechnic High School Graduation 1939.

Much to my sorrow my surfing ended when the breakwater was built to better protect the navy fleet homeported in Long Beach. The Tent City that belonged to my folks was torn down and they built in its place a seven-story apartment and hotel complex, Mariner and Mariner Annex. Dad used a room in the hotel to oversee the business.

My grandparents needed special care by this time, and my room in their home was to be given over to a full-time nurse. It was also decided that I needed more female influence in my life. After hours on the phone dad found a school that had a vacancy for a girl my age. The school was Brown's School for Girls. It was located in a beautiful orange grove in the foothills near Azusa, California. I loved it there and was very active in sports. I always loved competitive sports. I was there a year before returning to Long Beach to attend my senior year at Polytechnic High School, graduating in 1939.

My graduation day was held in Avalon on Catalina Island. The festivities ended with dancing in the Casino ballroom. Then it was back aboard the big steamship for the trip home.

After high school I spent a year at secretarial college. And nearly all of my adult life I have attended classes at Long Beach City College.

Water Sprite

Swimming by age three

Rowing my own skiff by age five

Sailing competitively at age six

Using a homemade diving mask at age six

Competitive swimmer at age seven

Water ballet at age seven

My first boat at age eight

Surfing and spearfishing at age six

Water taxi driver at age nine

Teen and adult years

- Aquaplaner
- Water skier
- Water polo
- Springboard diver
- Completed all Red Cross water craft classes
- Red Cross swimming instructor
- Red Cross lifeguard
- Skin diving instructor
- Scuba instructor

Appears in the Los Angeles Sportsman Show pool demonstrations

Appears in the Race for Life shows at the Pan Pacific Auditorium

Appears in the Los Angeles County Underwater Unit tank in the Little Wet School House

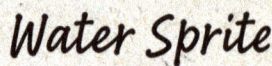

LA Sportsman Show, 1957

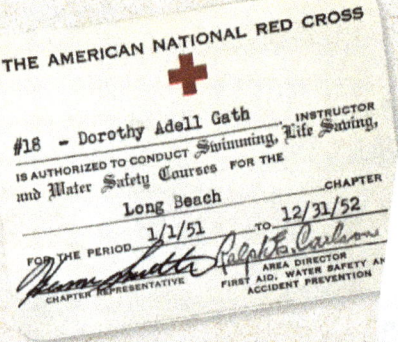

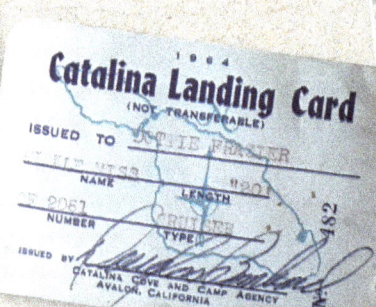

The Mariner 2, a 28 ft. yawl, 1928

The Invader, dad (Long Beach Pike roller coaster in the background) 1950s

The Fickle Miss (formerly named the 5 Ds)

The **Mariner 1**, a 28 ft. yawl, 1928

The Serenity of Sailing

I have always loved sailing. The quiet, peaceful tranquility while sailing downwind on a full reach, with the wind at our back, then tacking to sail up wind, hearing the wind whistling through the stays and rigging, with spray on our faces and heeled over so far that our rails were in the water. This kind of fun and excitement taught me to love the sea.

My dad kept a beautiful 28-foot Sea Bird yawl moored in a corner of Cherry Cove at Santa Catalina Island. As a small child I loved sitting on the stern watching the water below me. In the 1920s these waters were virtually untouched and in early mornings the water was clear as crystal and smooth as glass with not a ripple or movement on the surface.

I was mesmerized by the slow sway of the giant kelp leaves below my feet. I was now three years old and already fascinated by and well acquainted with the marine life in local waters.

The yawl was the replacement for the 21-foot sloop, *Dotadell*, which had proved too small for our little family during the numerous trips we took to the island. The yawl was called *Mariner*. We now spent even more time sailing and living over at Catalina on the boat.

By the time I was five I was sailing by myself in a sailing skiff in races at Alamitos Bay in the 'kiddy' division, hoping I'd win a first-place blue ribbon, which I did several times.

Birthday Boat

On my eighth birthday dad gave me a 13-foot rowboat called a clinker (clinker-built is also called lapstrake, a type of boat construction where the edges of the hull planks overlap). It had a three-horse Johnson outboard motor, two sets of oars and all the equipment necessary to rig the boat for sailing.

Mastering sailing and aquaplaning kept me busy every day. Aquaplaning was standing on a long surfboard and being towed through the water by my father in our outboard-powered skiff. In only a matter of a few weeks I could do a headstand on the board while underway, and so could my folks.

I learned to row single and tandem. Sculling took considerably longer to learn but after I'd finally mastered it, I used it as much as rowing. One oar is set in a single oarlock at the center of the stern. The operator stands holding the handle in one hand, moving the oar in a back and forth motion similar to a figure eight, which propels the boat forward. Distance swimming became a specialty and I could swim several miles without tiring, using at least five different strokes.

My time on the boat was a 24/7 school. I learned navigating, boxing a compass, tying knots in all size lines, docking, anchoring, rules for the ocean mariner and engine maintenance.

I loved learning all about fishing, marine life and fishing equipment. Then came the art of cleaning and the cooking of anything that came out of the ocean. I also learned about refueling engines and motors, adding oil, changing spark plugs, cleaning filters and changing a shear pin on the outboard. Dad was always adding to the long list of maintenance tasks.

Mariner 2, 1940

Life Aboard a Cruiser

When we had guests on board we really noticed how crowded *Mariner* was getting. Dad decided we needed a larger boat. He found a cruiser that would be more suitable for living aboard, providing more room for grandma and grandpa, mother and my sister to come with us. Dad immediately found a buyer for the yawl, bought the cruiser, and he and I moved aboard. He named her *Mariner 2*. Now we could make a faster trip to Catalina and the whole family could join in. For a long time afterwards I really missed the quiet of sailing.

Just about every weekend, holiday and during the summer dad and I spent the time on our new floating home at Catalina or anchored in Long Beach harbor. She was a 30-foot, raised deck, cabin cruiser divided into two areas. The cabin was on the lower level in the front half bow and the upper level at the rear or stern was called the cockpit where the wheelhouse or operating controls were situated. Directly above this area, attached to the front part of the cabin, were dual controls, allowing the operator to sit out in the open with 360-degree visibility.

The tiny bathroom or head had a minuscule washbasin and a toilet with a pump that brought in ocean water for flushing. There was no shower or bathtub and no hot water. At the stern (back) there was a swim step attached to the boat at the water's edge, about two feet wide and extending the width of the boat. This is where I soaped up all over, then jumped into the water, ranging from 58 to 73 degrees F. winter to summer, to rinse off. Taking a bath wasn't what I called fun!

My First Boat Jobs

Inside the Long Beach breakwater there was a fishing barge secured to big rocks close to where we anchored. It was a very popular place to visit for beachgoers, tourists and fishermen who didn't have boats. I walked out there on a daily basis, often helping less experienced fishermen bait hooks, rig poles, take fish off hooks, etc.

One day the barge owner asked me if I would like a job doing just what I had been doing and get paid an hourly rate. The offer was subject to dad's approval because I was 11 years old. My pay would be 10 cents an hour. Approval was granted, and soon I had a salary, tips and extra fish that the customers didn't want. I also cleaned catches for people who did not know what to do. I loved my job and could hardly wait for the night to end so I could go to work early in the morning.

Since dad and I were on the boat by ourselves most of the time, I had learned how to cook easy meals, make coffee for pop and prepare daily lunches. My boss on the barge asked me if I would like to work on his 38-foot fishing boat when it had to go on a run for live bait. He had already consulted dad and received the okay, hence my second job with the pay raise to 25 cents an hour was like a dream come true. All I had to do was keep the big coffeepot full and have sandwiches made on a moment's notice for the skipper and his two deckhands.

This was not an everyday job, occurring only when the two large live bait containers, floating and secured to the fishing barge, needed replenishing. On our boat I slept in an upper bunk where I could look out of the porthole, feel the wind on my face and hear the many seabirds squawking. When I was needed for work, usually before sunrise, one of the crew would come over to our boat, reach in the porthole and shake or poke me and tell me I had 10 minutes to get to work. I hurriedly dressed, woke dad to let him know that I was leaving and the boat would pull alongside for me to jump aboard.

We headed out to sea to hunt for schools of anchovy and sardine. Rough churned up water, in almost a circle, would indicate that we had located the baitfish that we needed. The area we were headed to was about three miles south of the lighthouse, unless a school was spotted before that. I made the big pot of coffee and took two steaming mugs up to the deckhands. I had to prepare the skipper's meal first, consisting of scrambled eggs, bacon and sweet rolls. It never varied. After the galley was clean I went up on deck to watch all the preparations necessary for the job at hand.

When the school was spotted the huge nets were played out slowly as we circled the fish, the nets were closed and the bottom was pulled together as the net was drawn in and piled on the deck. The small fish were churning madly in the net, which was now alongside the boat. The block and tackle was hooked up to the net, which was hoisted up and over the big bait tank filled with fresh seawater amid-ship at the stern. By releasing the bottom of the net it opened up and the bait fell into the water inside the bait tank. If the catch was the amount that the owner had ordered we could head back to port. If we needed more to fill the order the net was pulled aboard and we were off to look for more.

When we returned to port the bait was transferred from the tank into the containers tied to the barge. Each trip was different. Sometimes we lucked out and were back in just a few hours but other days we would hit rough seas, bad visibility and not a school of bait would be seen, which meant going out again the next day, weather permitting.

The owner of the barge had watched me going over and back to our cruiser in our small dinghy with a 5½-horsepower Johnson outboard. He had a 16-foot flat-bottom, wide-beam wooden skiff with a 10-horsepower outboard that he used to pick up passengers for the trip out to his fishing barge, about a quarter mile each way.

Some customers were young and surefooted enough to use the breakwater to walk out, but it was not a safe a thing to do. So I got the job with the raise in pay to 40 cents an hour to run a water taxi back and forth with passengers to the barge. Weekends I had full loads. I never got tired and I loved the job. I was 11 at the time.

'One of the Boys' on a Commercial Fishing Boat

This was my third year working on the *Georgia Ann*, an old 38-foot fantail diesel with an 18-foot plank off the bow for hunting and harpooning shark and swordfish. I had hired on as a cook, deckhand and assistant helmsman. The other deckhand was a former navy man in his 50s with red hair and a build for hard physical work. Our skipper had been a commercial fisherman all his life and was well known for his ocean experience and mechanical expertise. Our wages were based on shares; the skipper and boat received two shares while myself and the deckhand each received one share.

Three years earlier I had taken a secretarial job after graduating from business college. But I lasted just two months in my first desk job. It was not for me to sit in an office all day, five days a week, so I gave my two weeks' notice and started looking for employment more to my liking.

One night my dad called to see how the job hunting was going. After telling him that I had not yet found anything, he asked if I would like to work on a commercial fishing boat. A friend of his, a boat skipper, had called to say that his deckhand was in the hospital and he had not been able to find a replacement. Did he know of anyone with experience who might be interested in shipping out immediately?

Dad said he knew someone. The skipper was elated until he learned that the person mentioned was female. "No, no," said the skipper, "I am not running a school and it is bad luck to have a woman aboard." Dad explained that he was referring to me, his daughter, who had been raised on boats and lived on, around or in the ocean most of her life. She had been trained by him in all aspects of maritime life: mechanics, navigation, fishing, cooking, repairs and was an excellent skin diver who could put lobsters and abalone on the menu whenever they anchored near islands. Dad assured the skipper that I would sign on at a moment's notice.

I was soon interviewed by the skipper, then had to meet the deckhand to gain his approval. I wore bulky clothes to hide my boobs, no make-up, a knit watch hat; nothing to look female. I got the job and the *Georgia Ann* became my new home for the next two months.

Since I was the youngest and had excellent long-distance vision, one of my duties was to spend time in the crow's nest (situated at the top of the mast above the flying bridge), looking for fish on the surface. On this trip, we were hunting for sharks to harpoon. My job was to look for the telltale signs of dorsal and tailfins.

Back then, shark liver oil was used in medicines. The only part of the shark with any value in those days was their huge livers. One liver of a good-sized shark could fill a 50-pound bucket. The rest of the carcass would be discarded overboard.

By the time we had canned enough shark livers to make a profit, the skipper ordered us to head for the east end of Catalina Island. After another two weeks of successful harpooning here it was time to head back to the mainland with our livers, pick up supplies, our pay, see our families, get a hot shower, then get ready to turnaround for the next trip, this time for Broadbill Swordfish, a much more difficult fish to hunt, but very lucrative if caught.

Editor's note: *Shark liver oil has been used for centuries in folk remedies to promote healing of wounds and for respiratory and digestive problems. It is still promoted today as a dietary supplement. Unsubstantiated claims are made that the oil can be used to treat cancer, HIV, radiation illness, swine flu and the common cold. Shark liver oil is still used in some moisturizing skin lotions and hemorrhoid medications. At the time of this writing, much is being done around the world to help conserve shark populations from decline and/or collapse, a result of overfishing, including wasteful shark finning for soup and folklore remedies.*

The Chum, 1946

Fisherman's Landing, Pier Point, 1948

Galley Cook

24/7 Galley Cook and Deckhand

In My Own Words • Boat Life

Storm at Sea

From Long Beach I boarded a bus for San Diego at 5 am to meet my skipper and our other deckhand aboard the *Georgia Ann*. Our clearance papers and fishing permits for Mexican waters had been taken care of the previous day by the skipper, Dick.

I got my sea bag stowed and a cup of hot coffee and we shoved off, headed south down the coast. I took the helm. The skipper and Red, the deckhand, hit their bunks, tired from icing the holds, loading food, water and fuel for as long as a month at sea.

We cruised all day before pulling into a small cove and dropping the hook. I prepared supper and we tried some fishing, with enough luck for fish to be on the menu the next night. The sun had barely gone down when two tired fishermen and one fisherwoman headed for their sleeping bags, knowing that daylight was coming up fast and a big day lay ahead.

We had been told that Longfin Tuna, also known as Albacore, were running further south about 30 miles offshore. I fixed a big breakfast of coffee, bacon, eggs, toast and fruit and we weighed anchor. We dropped in our trolling lines and heading south to hunt for these elusive fish.

After three days of cruising there was still no sign of the fish. On the fourth day our stern trolling line got a strike. We had four lines on each side of the boat and two astern.

Sitting on the flying bridge at the helm, I immediately put the boat in a wide circle. Almost instantly several of the other lines took hits. We were hauling in good-sized Albacore as fast as we possibly could. I put the boat on automatic control so that it would continue circling, and I went down to do what I could to help bring in more fish. I was too small to land any fish over 15 pounds, so when one of the boys felt that they had a light fish on they handed me the line and I would bring that one in myself.

We landed and iced down a good number of 15-plus pounders and then the bite quit. We got the fish in the hold, cleaned up the deck and headed at least a mile out, but no luck spotting another boil of fish feeding on the surface.

During the next two weeks the weather stayed nice and the ocean remained placid. Schools of fish were hit and miss, but we still added catches to our ice hold. We knew by now that this trip would allow each of us to end up with a nice paycheck.

Since it was calm with no wind, we took three-hour watches and just drifted, each getting some shut-eye. After the much-needed rest we headed out again and five miles out we hit another small school. We lucked out this time as we had almost filled our ice hold. Now the ocean started getting rough. We realized that we were experiencing the beginning of a Mexican chubasco, or ocean hurricane. (See note below.)

The wind increased, creating deep troughs in the waves that the 38-foot boat would plow down, burying the 18-foot harpooning plank in the swell. Then we went high up the wave and smashed down the other side. The plank couldn't take that kind of treatment for long. The cable holding it snapped, and the plank came crashing back against the starboard side, breaching the cabin.

The skipper hollered to me up on the bridge to keep the boat from broaching or turning over. He said all bilge pumps were on but the water was pouring into the cabin, so he in our deckhand were lying on the bunk opposite the hole and holding a mattress with their feet against it trying to keep the water from coming in. They couldn't help relieve me until the sea calmed down. I was too busy doing my job to worry much, even though waves were breaking over the bridge.

I was chilled to the bone, soaked to my skin, sore, thirsty, hungry and needed a trip to the head. After another hard hour on the helm the seas calmed down and I finally relaxed my tensed and hurting arms and legs. Pretty soon the boys could come out of the cabin and check for damage.

The skipper had had the foresight to use his cable cutters to free the plank from the boat when it broke loose. The bilge pump probably saved our lives. It kept the water out of the engine room and we never lost power during the storm. Because the engine never lost a beat, I was able to work the waves, riding them when necessary and always heading the bow straight in, to avoid being caught broadside.

After the waves subsided we shut down and just drifted, taking a much-needed rest. I changed to dry clothes, got the coffee pot boiling and made snacks. I checked our compass and figured a new course for our homeport.

It was another two full days and nights before we could see land, which sure looked good to me. It was early morning when we got to the unloading docs and emptied our hold. I packed my gear, did the necessary hosing down and galley cleanup. I was ready to step off the minute we got to the tie-ups.

I grabbed a 20-pound Albacore, threw it into a big ice bag and tied a nylon line around it through the gills and mouth so I could carry it with my sea bag over my shoulder. I grabbed a cab to the bus station, where I shocked a lot of passengers as I got aboard the bus for home looking like something very dirty and not female. I didn't feel like one either. I just thanked God I was still alive.

Editor's note: *A chubasco is a sudden sea storm with thunder and lightning that occurs during the rainy season along the Pacific Coast of Mexico, in the Sea or Cortez, Central America and South America. The word originates form the Portuguese, chuva, meaning rain.*

The Georgia Ann, 1946

Dottie, 16 years old

Trailblazer: The Extraordinary Life of Diving Pioneer Dottie Frazier

Catalina Island

My happy home - peaceful Catalina

Dottie & her sister Jeanne, 1937

The Magic of Catalina

When business slacked off and dad had plenty of help at the office, we headed across the Catalina Channel with supplies to last for a week or so. We sat up on the cabin of our cruiser where dual controls were located, giving us a 360-degree view. On some days visibility was so perfect that the island looked only a few miles away.

On one trip we were sitting up on top of the cabin when dad noticed a black schooner at least a mile off our starboard bow, heading towards the mainland. He remarked "that looks like the *Black Witch*. I said "No, it's the *Gypsy Girl*." "How do you know that?" he asked. "Because I can read it on the side plates up on the mast stays," I replied. Dad was stunned as he could barely see the nameplate, let alone any lettering on it.

Soon afterwards he took me to his optometrist for an eye examination, which showed that I had acute farsightedness. This answered the puzzle of the trouble that I had been having in school learning to read. At the ripe old age of seven I began wearing glasses when necessary.

During the 26-mile crossing of the channel we had the opportunity to see lots of whales and porpoise so thick you could just about walk across on their backs. Sharks were plentiful, swimming lazily along with their tails swinging back and forth. An occasional Broadbill Swordfish with its dorsal and tailfin cutting the water like a knife was observed. Huge, bulky, shiny Ocean Sunfish weighing several hundred pounds floated without a care in the world with their one long fin sticking out and waving to us as we passed by.

On one of our Catalina trips I learned about the constellations and stars at night when dad and I sat on the top of the cabin enjoying the beauty of the sky without the lights from the city. I learned which planets and stars would guide us where we needed to go and how the stars keep changing their positions as the world keep turning and seasons begin to change. There was always something new to learn.

Close Call in a Cave

One night dad woke me after midnight and said, "Let's get dressed in something warm and then come up on deck as soon as your can." It was a dark, moonless sky, and with only our flashlights as our running lights we took off in our 13-foot clinker skiff that was powered by a small outboard. We headed out of the cove where we were anchored then crossed the Isthmus Harbor of Catalina Island to the far cliffs that rose blackly from the rocky shore.

It was an extremely low minus tide, and many caves were exposed at the water's edge. One in particular seemed larger than many that we had passed. Dad shut off the outboard and we put the oars in the locks. He slowly rowed into the pitch-black entrance to the cave. The cave was about 10-feet high and close to the same width, and extended back about 20 feet. The depth of the water wasn't much over three feet.

When we turned off our lights we were spellbound at the fantastic sight before our eyes. There were abalone all over the walls, as well as many varieties of starfish, sea anemones and seaweed in florescent colors. Looking down in the shallow water we could see many species of small fish, as well as crabs, small lobsters, octopus, eels, scallops and sea urchins. There was an abundance of sea life, some of which were unknown to us.

Engrossed with this cornucopia of sea life, we stayed too long in the cave, unaware of the surge and incoming tide. It had been necessary to duck our heads to gain entry, but now the boat was higher than the top of the cave opening. The grim reality of our predicament dictated some extreme measures. The outboard was too high, so it was hastily removed and stowed in the bottom of the boat. It wasn't enough. We lifted some heavy rocks into the skiff, lowering it further into the rising water.

We managed to free the bow from the cave opening, and only then, pushing against the ceiling of the cave from the stern, we were able to inch our way to safety.

I still shudder to think what could have happened had we been unable to free the skiff. Steep cliffs, no beach, and a swim of several miles in inky darkness back to our floating home. Only after safely reaching the *Mariner* did I have time to think back at what could have been a tragic end to out nocturnal adventure.

I was a cold, happy, tired, seven-year-old when I climbed into my top bunk that night and gave thanks to someone watching over us.

Island Meals

Our meals while anchored at Catalina Island consisted mostly of fish, lobster and abalone with fresh vegetables that dad and I both loved. The fish were easy to catch from the boat but lobster and abalone were a little harder to hunt. For the lobster we set special traps baited with a skeleton of the fish that we had for supper. Dad had made the trap out of wood and wire screen, about three-feet by four-feet with a funnel opening at the top. Lobsters would crawl in the top to get at the bait but couldn't crawl back out again. We set the trap at night in a rocky area on the bottom in 15 to 20 feet of water. There were lines attached to the trap and also to a float on the surface.

After it had been down overnight when the 'bugs' (lobsters) feed, the trap would be pulled up and the contents dumped into our boat. Sometimes we also found crabs and even an occasional eel. One time Dad hauled the trap up and over the side into the boat, unhooked the door and dumped the contents out. I don't remember which one of us dove over the side first, he on the port and me on the starboard. The trap had about eight Moray Eels in it. They had eaten most of the legs and feelers off of all of the lobsters, but we managed to salvage the tails. The eels didn't stay long in the boat; we felt lucky that we hadn't been part of their meal!

At Catalina Island we always anchored close to shore so I could swim to shore and collect seashells while dad could keep his eye on me from the boat.

One of my favorite things to do was to get my little fishing pole, set up my line and hooks, and tell daddy I was going to catch our dinner, (which was easy, as there were lots of fish around the boat, and they were always hungry). In the afternoon when the wind came up was dad would give me another sailing lesson in our little 7-foot dinghy, which I dearly loved.

When time allowed we would pick different coves where we could pull the skiff up on to the beach. There were many animal trails leading into the hills, so after picking one, we would head out to explore. We found many abandoned mines, some Indian or Mexican artifacts, ran into feral pigs, deer, buffalo, goats, fox and even hunted several rattlesnakes, which we took back for supper.

Before heading back to our home on our boat we always visited the clam beds in the shallow water at the sandpit, which jutted out just beyond the wreck. In no more than 15 minutes we had our homemade cloth bags full of two-inch Cockle Clams. Dad made delicious clam chowder as soon as we got to the boat and we had it for our supper that night.

All around the island we would see Flying Fish. These fish swim very fast just under the surface of the water and suddenly jump up and skim on the top for incredible distances, just as if it was flying. At night tourists could pay to watch this sight from a large launch that was rigged with a powerful searchlight, which attracted the fish towards the boat. More often than not the fish would land among the passengers creating a mad scramble to catch this 18-inch wonder, which is considered to be a delicacy among islanders. Our method for hunting them was to hang a lantern over the side of our boat at night when we were anchored. In a very short time one would swim into the lighted area and I would spear it with my three-pronged pole spear. The islanders were right; this was a real delicacy.

Hunting Abalone

We were very familiar with the different species of abalone, the Black being the most common and less desirable. It is the smallest and found in shallow water, also at low tide, out of water attached to rocks, and can live for several hours without being submerged. The other three types found in this area, from a few feet to over 100 feet, are the Green, Pink, and White (also called the Sorenson). Abalone is a mollusk, or sea snail, with a hard shell on one side and a muscular suction foot on the other. They attach themselves to rocks, often in tight hiding places that made it difficult to get at them.

Dad devised a special method of hunting abalone. He made an underwater 'look box' with waterproofed wood sides with a piece of glass glued to the bottom. The top was left open and placed on the surface of the water at the rear of the boat. The observer would kneel on the rear seat of the skiff, leaning over with his or her head and face almost in the box, which floated. This made it possible to see anything on the bottom, looking as if was just a foot or so away from you.

Dad also designed a special abalone pole. He fabricated four sections of five-foot wooden dowel, each screwing onto the other, with a 12-inch tire iron modified to a spear shaped point attached to the main shaft. Depending on the water depth, we'd know how many of the sections to use.

This was a two-person job; one at the oars and the other positioned at the stern of the boat watching the bottom for abalone. When one was spotted the oarsman took directions from the spotter to put the stern directly over it. We usually worked with two of the sections attached the third to add in case we needed extra length.

After positioning over the abalone we would slowly push the pole down to the bottom, placing the head of the spear between the rock and the abalone, then twisting the blade to break the abalone's suction to the rock. The abalone then falls off and can be speared and brought to the surface. Cleaning and preparing lobster and abalone for dinner were other lessons I learned.

Shark Rodeo

The West End of Catalina Island was very remote and visited mostly by boat. In the small settlement on shore you could buy groceries, first-aid supplies, sandwiches, soft drinks, ice cream, etc. A bar was available for drinks. There was a mechanic shop, a place to shower, and on the end of the short pier was the office where owners of yachts could rent boat moorings. This was the favorite place for the rich and famous, including movie stars.

This spot on the island is at the narrowest point, at only one-eight of a mile from one side to the other. The south side was called Catalina Harbor and a large portion of the bay nearest shore is very shallow for about 100 yards. Dad and I made frequent hikes there, and on one of these we saw the bay filled with shark fins protruding above the surface.

They looked to be mostly Leopard Sharks, which are considered to be a harmless species. We thought they might be there for mating. They were moving slowly and lazily along in all directions. Dad had me wait on shore while he waded into the water up to his waist. They didn't seem to be alarmed by his presence, so he grabbed the dorsal fin of one cruising by and was towed around for several minutes. Then it was my turn. I followed the same procedure and we took rides on four or five different sharks. It was great fun.

Exploring Wrecks

In deeper water at Catalina Harbor there was the wreck of an old three-masted sailing schooner. She was lying on her side at such an angle that her starboard rail was low to the water, with the port rail at the high side of the ship. The masts were still intact and leaned out over the water. Someone had tied a long line from to one of the yardarms to the rail. If one was physically able (and we were) to climb to the high side, take a good grip of the end of the line, they could swing way out over the water and drop off with a big splash. What a thrill! Even dad loved to do it and we spent so much time enjoying our new sport that we wore ourselves out.

We also explored another old ship's hull in the water, which was rotted away to the waterline. We found lots of interesting sea life that made the wreck their home. There were crabs, lobster, octopus, starfish, sea urchins and eels among the inhabitants.

Speaking with some of the old-timers who had been around the area for many years, we found out that this old ship was all that remained of the once-notorious *Ningpo*. The *Ningpo* was launched in 1753 in the city of Fu Chau, China, as a three-masted, 138-foot junk. She was said to be the "fastest and best equipped vessel afloat in Chinese waters," and it wasn't long before the merchant trader turned into a smuggler, pirate ship and prison ship.

After many high-seas adventures, the *Ningpo* arrived in Southern California in 1913 as a floating attraction. In 1917 she was towed to Catalina Harbor for display. In 1935 she burned to the waterline in Catalina Harbor, perhaps while serving as a movie set.

Some items once aboard the *Ningpo,* as well as woodcarvings made from timbers from the ship, can still be seen on display in the Catalina Island Museum in the Avalon Casino.

The *Ningpo*

Glover's Reef, Honduras
photos by Barb Allen

Skin Diving

My First Dive

One morning while anchored in a beautiful little bay close to a rocky shore, dad called me out of the cabin and told me that he had just dropped the coffeepot over the side of the boat while rinsing it. He had a bad cold and didn't want to make it worse by diving in to retrieve the pot.

I could see the pot in the crystal clear water just 15 feet below. I was a good swimmer, could dive off the highest part of the boat, swim down the anchor line eight or 10 feet, do surface and porpoise dives, but 15 feet deep? No way.

Dad convinced me that I could go down and recover his coffeepot. When I was in the water he handed me a small anchor with a line attached to it. He told me that when he let go of the line that it would pull me down to the bottom and land right alongside of the pot and all I had to do was grab it and head for the surface. I took a big breath and the anchor took me right where dad said it would. Even with the blurred vision I could see the pot. I grabbed it and headed back up.

It wasn't too long after that dive that I was making lots of dives at that depth, picking up shells and salvaging things that had fallen off other boats. I mentioned to dad one day that I wished I could see better when I was on the bottom.

The next week daddy seemed busier than usual and didn't seem to have any time for me. But later he came over to where I was fishing and put a funny piece of an old fire hose up to my face. He did some marking and measuring, came back several times to repeat what he had done the first time. Finally that piece of hose fit over my eyes and nose. He shaved, cut, marked and repeated this several more times until it actually fit the contours of my face.

The next step was to put a piece of circular glass that he had cut out of a broken window into one side of the hose. With tape, glue, more tape and some rubber inner tube strips on each side to hold it to my face, presto, a faceplate, also called a diving mask!

The first time that I wore my mask was like a miracle. I could see everything under water as clear as if I were on the surface. I could see all sizes of the fish that I knew so well, with all of their vivid, beautiful colors. I could see the abalones attached to the rocks and the lobsters hidden in the rocky crevices, along with the ugly, scary-looking Moray Eels. There were starfish and Sea Cucumbers on every rock, with scallops and spiny Sea Urchins everywhere. Eel Grass, Sea Fans, and kelp trees rising from the ocean bottom to spread out on the surface like a giant carpet, all making up the most unbelievable, underwater forest and gardens that anyone could imagine.

From this time forward, this became my world. New discoveries presented themselves daily amid this constantly changing underwater wonderland. It also became a gourmet smorgasbord of seafood delicacies for pop and me to choose from when planning our meals. I could hardly wait for dad to finally get the masks leak-proof and more comfortable.

It wasn't long before I could hunt abalone, prying them off a rock and bringing two or three up on every dive. One of the owners on a nearby fancy yacht stopped by in his speedboat where I was diving and asked if he could buy some abalone from me. I took his order and delivered them within 30 minutes. I even got paid extra for taking them out of the shell so before I knew it I had more orders than I could fill.

I did sell some lobster, but they were harder to find so I stuck mainly to abalone. Getting lobster or 'bugs,' as they were called, took a lot of practice to be fast enough to grab them. But after a little more than a year I was even faster than dad.

From Look Box to Double-Rubber Arbalete

While dad was busy fine-tuning our masks we continued to hunt abalone using the glass-bottom box and abalone pole. On one of these trips I was absorbed in viewing the ocean floor from the look box while dad handled the oars. As we passed over a sandy area I spotted a huge halibut partially buried in the sand. Without speaking or raising my head I motioned to dad to move the boat astern slightly over where I was kneeling at the look box, ahead and to the left.

I positioned the pole with its sharpened tire iron tip straight up-and-down. With all the force I could manage I shoved the pole downward. My aim was just to hit the fish. The spear tip went through its stomach and into the hard sand beneath.

I had no idea what to expect. When the pole started rotating around and around rapidly, I yelled for dad to help me. He grabbed the pole not knowing what I had just hit, holding the pole firmly down so that it couldn't move. The fish, trying to get away, did nothing more than go around in a circle and the faster it went the closer it came up to the boat finally crashing into the keel and knocking itself out. We got it on board and then just sat staring at this 30-pound halibut.

From that time on and up to today I still am partial to halibut steaks.

After dad and I came up more than a few times with both hands bleeding from the sharp spines of the lobster and skinning our knuckles against the rocks, we decided our next piece of equipment would be a good heavy pair of gloves for both of us.

I was practicing spearing fish with a three-prong hand spear. I didn't have too much luck for quite some time but then I started using a Hawaiian sling and started hitting some fair-sized species in the six- to eight-pound range. I rarely went in the water without my spear and became quite proficient at depths up to 20 feet. As I got older I hunted much larger fish in deeper water and graduated to a double-rubber arbalete spear gun. I considered myself quite an expert upon spearing my first Yellowtail and White Seabass.

Diving for Coins

One day I was swimming by what was called the dinghy dock where people from the yachts out in the harbor would row in and tie their shore boat up and pick it up when they had finished their business ashore. A lady had just crawled aboard her little skiff and yelled, "Oh, I dropped my purse overboard." I made a fast dive and grabbed her purse off the bottom, surfaced and handed it to her. She couldn't thank me enough and gave me all of the change she had, which was about three dollars.

From that time for the rest of the summer, I had many people who would come by our boat to ask if they could hire me to recover some item they had dropped to the bottom. Most of the boats moored in the first three or four rows were in water not over 20-feet deep, which was an easy dive for me. Dad had bought me one of the first pair of swim fins we had even heard about. I think they were made by Churchill. My second pair was Duck Feet.

I had quite a little business going on recovering everything from anchors, to wallets and with the fins and my new toy, a snorkel, I was constantly out scanning the bottom under every boat. The snorkel was a piece of hose about two feet long, one end held in the mouth to breathe through, the other end tucked under the strap by the ear, that holds the mask on the face.

You could glide over the surface of the water looking below you and breathing from the snorkel without lifting your head up except for once in a while, to get your bearing, and see where you wanted to go. Dad would get the biggest kick out of checking all my findings each time I came back to the boat. By this time I was towing an inflated inner tube with a sack tied on the inside where I could put all the treasures that I found. I had a line tied to it that allowed me to tow it behind me as I snorkeled along.

When we were moored at the Isthmus in close to the shore, I used to watch the huge passenger ship from Avalon slowly make its way up to the pier. Most of the passengers were in the bow throwing coins to a bunch of local kids in the water by the ship, swimming and yelling, "Throw us a penny or nickel!" They would dive under the water and grab the coin as it slowly sank. Dad, knowing that I had wanted to get in the game for quite a while, finally gave me the go ahead. I grabbed my new mask and went off to join the kids.

I was the only one out of about 20 kids who had a diving mask and none had ever even seen one before. In no time I had more coins than I could hold in my mouth, which was where we had to put them. I hurried back to our boat, spit them out into my dinghy and back for another mouthful. The Avalon ship was a daily arrival so I was by the pier waiting for it to come in every day that we were at the island, all summer. By the third time I dove for the coins I had made a cloth bag, attached it to my trunks with safety pins and didn't have to hold the money in my mouth anymore. The other kids copied my idea real fast.

When it was necessary to go down to the little city of Avalon, at the other end of the island, to pick up some much-needed supplies, I got to see how the big kids greet the big Catalina steamer from the mainland. There were hundreds of passengers lining the rails and they threw mostly 50-cent and 25-cent coins, and the occasional silver dollar. I had to be able to swim faster, dive deeper and even fight for a place in which to tread water. I was still the only girl, but by then well experienced, so I did all right. My little savings account was looking pretty good.

1952 Dive meet first prize electric ray

Diving Derbies

One of my diving buddies called me one evening and asked if I would enter a Diving Derby as his partner. It was being sponsored by some of the manufacturers of diving gear and was open to anyone. Jack and I signed up right away. There were a number of different categories from which to choose. The contest was seven days running and you could enter as many times as you got something worth entering. All of Palos Verde and as far south as Costa Mesa was the hunting area. We chose to stay in the PV area and entered catches such as abalone, lobster, fish, sharks and rays. Jack and I hunted every day for five days without finding anything worth entering.

On our last day I had been diving for several hours but hadn't seen anything larger that I had already entered until I spotted a good-sized ray, which I didn't recognize. I dove to where he was swimming lazily along the bottom. Deciding that he might be a winner, I took careful aim and pulled the trigger of my double-rubber arbalete. The shot was good, but not lethal, and the startled ray took off. Fortunately the barb held. It took me for quite a ride before I was able to surface. I had a considerable amount of line out and started reeling it in.

Jack hollered, asking what I had speared. I told him it was a ray but I had never seen one like it before. He came right over but also failed to recognize the species. He told me to keep reeling it in and that he would help me to get it up over the large float that we had with us to contain our catch. When the ray was within reach Jack grabbed the tail, after ascertaining that this particular species didn't have the tail barbs as most rays do. Well I hadn't heard anyone scream louder and he sure let go of that ray fast, saying, "NOW I know what that is, it is an electric ray!"

Later we carefully loaded it into the trunk of the car and drove to a weigh-in station and registered it in the ray division, where it took a first prize. I also got a first in the lobster division. The prizes were set up for men and since I was the only female diver I had few choices that I could use. The judges and committees finally listened to my complaints about having to dive with only male competitors so after a few years a women's division was formed. However, when the prizes were awarded to us they were items such as bathing suits, beach sandals, hats, towels, etc. In the male division prizes included wetsuits, spearguns, fins, masks, floats, etc. There were seldom more than three or four females competing for the first several years, but we never received equal prizes. Male domination I'd say.

During these contests I became well acquainted with Dr. Nelson 'Doc' Mathison, Herb Sampson, 'Big Jim' Christiansen, Jack Ward, Gene Davies and countless others, some of whom became well known for their diving accomplishments. I entered every derby I could and took a good share of the prizes for many years.

Look Before You Leap

On a trip to Catalina Island, the water was so warm that our new wetsuits were not needed, for a change. We spent the day in and out of the water using mask, snorkel and fins to get our abalone and some nice-sized bugs (lobster).

After sunning on deck and diving repeatedly off the cabin into the water, and then another hour of sunning, we decided to dive one more time off the top of the cabin, and then it would be time to head home.

As I was about to dive I looked down and saw in the water a very strange object that looked like a rope about three feet beneath the surface. It looked to be about 10 to 15 feet in length and about one-inch thick. It was nearly transparent with black dots about three inches apart on the inside.

Ignorance is bliss, or so they say, and I dove in, right through the middle of whatever it was. When I came up to the surface I was screaming, a result of the pain I was experiencing. I was pulled aboard a nearby fishing boat with tangles of jellyfish-like strings clinging to my body.

As I tried to push the strings off my hands felt they were on fire. The skipper turned on the hose that was used to fill the bait tank and proceeded to wash the strings off of me. He said he thought they were some kind of jellyfish or perhaps jellyfish eggs.

The pain didn't quit until the skipper got a bottle of ammonia and a pot cleaner pad. I was rubbed down thoroughly, until the pain slowly dissipated. I had large welts that looked like I had been burned. I was very uncomfortable until I finally got home and iced myself down.

Now I will never forget the old adage, "Look before you leap, and know what you are leaping into."

Editor's note: *What Dottie encountered was mostly likely a siphonophore, a invertebrate colonial animal that usually lives in cold, deep waters and can swim independently in the water column. The Portuguese Man o' War, known for its powerful sting, is also a type of siphonophore.*

1956. Dottie and her dive buddy dog.

Robbed by a Seal

On one trip to Catalina Island I had one of the closest calls of my diving experiences. Our boat was small, but a very seaworthy cruiser. All of the six divers aboard, including me, were experience skin divers. Our objective that day was what we called "meat runs," meaning we all had near-empty freezers at home and needed to hunt whatever we could catch, spear or grab.

Our first dive was in a remote area near the West End. Soon, each of us had our limit of abalone and lobster. We had not seen many fish big enough to spear, so we pulled anchor to cruise to a more productive area.

It was a beautiful warm day and the visibility underwater was exceptionally good. We rounded a rocky point two miles east and came across a kelp bed; a prime place for spearing fish as they hide under the giant leaves floating on the surface.

By the time we anchored, two of the boys had already jumped overboard and were on their way to the kelp, hoping to get lucky and surprise a big Yellowtail or White Seabass, which had been showing up recently. I decided to have a bite of my lunch before diving, so I was the last one in the water. I decided to check a different spot, figuring that the guys had probably spooked the fish in the area that they were working. I headed out to a reef that I had spotted not far from where we anchored.

On my first dive I speared a nice Calico Bass, about two pounds, and put it on my stringer, which was attached to a belt around my waist. The stringer had about 10 hooks like large safety pins to stick through the gills and out the mouth of the fish. If you are lucky, you can fill all 10 hooks with nice fish before heading back to the boat.

I had a hunting method of diving to the bottom, finding a large sea urchin and smashing it, using the large diver's knife strapped to my leg. This was called baiting. I would pick an open area between lots of rocks and seaweed, protected area that were home for many different species and sizes of fish. It only took a couple of minutes for my prey to get the scent of food and emerge from holes and crevices. I could pick and choose which fish I wanted to take home.

I would spear one, head to the surface, string my catch and head back down for another shot. When I had all the fish I could safely swim with, I headed back to the boat, lifting my head now and then to take a bearing and stay on course. I got within hailing distance when I heard shouting. I raised my head and saw two of the divers on deck waving their arms. Then something struck me in the middle of my body on the right side. I felt myself rolling a couple of times, then there was nothing but black.

I regained consciousness lying on a mattress on deck, covered with a blanket and hurting all over. I no longer had my wetsuit on and I was taped all around my ribcage. Luckily for me, the skipper was a Red Cross first-aid instructor and knew what to do for broken ribs.

I had foolishly allowed the stringer of fish to trail alongside my body, which attracted a big male seal. He rushed me so fast grabbing the stringer that when making a sharp turn away he plowed into me, sending me rolling over and over, like a cork. He knocked every ounce of air out of my lungs. The fellows on the boat were only 60 feet away and saw what happened. When I started sinking they dove right in and got me back aboard.

X-rays later proved that the initial diagnosis was correct; I had two broken and two cracked ribs. I was lucky that the boys were back on the boat before me, saw what happened and took the initiative to rescue me.

This was a lesson I learned and never forgot. From then on I kept my catches away from my body. Now I used an inflated inner tube with a catch sack hanging down the inside. I also carried a light line on the tube that can be used as an anchor line, either tied to kelp or attached to a small weight.

I still feel insulted to have been robbed by a seal!

1956. Darrell, David, Daniel, Dottie and Donald.

Trailblazer: The Extraordinary Life of Diving Pioneer Dottie Frazier

The War Years

The year I graduated from high school my mom and her husband moved up to the mountains around Big Bear. I looked forward to heading to the slopes to snow ski as often as possible.

However, my plans changed when I fell in love. I met Don Gath at a friend's home in 1938. He worked at a gas station. I became Mrs. Donald M. Gath in 1940. Friends and family attended the wedding at the First Methodist Church in Long Beach. For a wedding present, my dad gave us a two-year rental of one of his properties. Within a year I had a beautiful son, whom we named Darrell Thomas. Two years later along came Donald Lee. My Mom babysat and I worked part-time as a waitress. Don got a job at a bigger gas station and we moved to a larger apartment.

When the war broke out, after the bombing of Pearl Harbor by the Japanese in 1941, both Don and I got jobs at Douglas Aircraft. He was a motor mechanic and I was a "Rosie the Riveter." It was a shock to me when Don and two of his buddies joined the Marines. He went to Camp Pendleton, San Diego, for training.

I had been saving every penny I could since graduating from high school, and now I had to find another place to live. After much looking I found a place that needed a lot of work. I told the owner it was overpriced, but I would be willing to buy it for a lower price and do the work myself. There was some hemming and hawing by the owner, but as I turned to walk out of the house after making my final offer, he relented. I got the house for $6,500. It was every cent I had in my savings account. Don could not believe what I did!

We started camping in the house, making repairs. But after only three months, Don was deployed overseas. Mom, Dad, my sister and her husband and many of my diving buddies helped me in every imaginable way to make me and my young sons as comfortable as possible.

In additional to working part-time, I was doing a lot of much-needed work on the house and began building a workshop in the garage. My grandparents and parents gave me gifts of tools and supplies, and soon I had a fully equipped workspace where I could handle tasks such as electrical, plumbing, carpentry and roofing. A long-time friend traded services with me. I taught his three kids how to swim and he helped me replace furnaces and ducting in my house.

I bought that 21-year-old frame house with a garage-over apartment in 1940. I paid for it primarily with the money earned working on a commercial fishing boat.

As of 2019, I still live in the same house, a few blocks from the ocean that I love so much.

Dottie May shows off her garage full of tools, where the 78-year-old can fix almost anything. May was recently inducted into the Women Divers Hall of Fame. Leo Hetzel / Press-Telegram

Building a New Life

The boys and I were happy and enjoying our remodeled home. Then one day I answered the front door bell to find two men in uniform. They informed me that a mortar shell at Iwo Jima had wounded my dear, wonderful Don. Most of his platoon had been wiped out. The injured had been sent to a hospital, Don among them. All I knew was that he was in critical condition, but did not know what the injuries were. I was in shock for many weeks, waiting to learn more.

Finally I received a letter. Don's injuries were one leg off above the knee, and serious injuries to one wrist and hand, one eye, his nose and his jaw. Don was headed to the Mare Island naval facility and hospital in Vallejo, Northern California. He faced an uncertain future of rebuilding his shattered body. I would be notified when I could visit him. I didn't tell the kids; they were so young and adored their daddy. My Mom was ready to move in and care for the kids as soon as I could head to Vallejo.

I arrived at Vallejo four months later, but was told that Don did not want to see me. He could not talk and was limited to communicating with his one good hand. I was told that his recovery could take years. In the meantime, I was given lodging in a Quonset hut. I began serving as a hospital volunteer six days a week. I helped amputees in the pool. Eventually Don relented and I was allowed short visits with my husband.

Every other month I returned to Long Beach to visit Darrell and Donny and relieve my mom of childcare duties. After a year of shuttling between Long Beach and Vallejo, the doctor told me that Don did not have the will to live, and that seeing me and thinking of the boys only made matters worse. He said I should return to Long Beach and rebuild my life without Don. It was hard for me to believe that this is what the doctor said. But after discussing it with my parents, I consented.

Editor's note: Don eventually recovered and was discharged from the hospital. He was given a specially modified car and enjoyed driving. He died a short time later, the result of an accident. Darrell and Donald Gath attended his funeral.

A Second Marriage

I found myself alone with two sons, trying to be both a father and a mother to them. Nor did I have a job. I decided that I must find a way to support us and still be able to remain at home and raise my kids. I hit upon the plan of running a boarding house from my home, using many of the carpentry, wiring and plumbing skills taught to me by my dad.

My church pastor helped by introducing me to several women who knew out-of-town families who had teenaged boys. These older boys had been offered jobs in Long Beach and needed weekday housing. Soon I added more boys to the house as boarders. I supplemented our income by waitressing at night, and I helped feed my sons and boarders by spearfishing, fishing and hunting.

While running the boarding house, I taught my boys all the skills I knew that a father would be teaching them. By the time Darrell turned eight he was already an accomplished

diver for his age and spent several times a week after school in the ocean at the foot of our street. He rarely returned home without something he had speared for our supper. I also managed to get a few dives in during the week and kept our big freezer filled up with fish and shellfish.

In 1951 I married Jake Frazier and had two more boys, David and then Daniel. But I soon divorced and found myself raising four boys alone! It was actually easier than I thought it would be, thanks to the fantastic skills and self-reliance instilled in me by my dad when I was a child.

I did almost all of the work on my home myself, including building the fences, rebuilding the porch, removing a wall to enlarge the kitchen, hanging new doors, repairing and raising the foundation, tiling, plumbing, electrical, paneling and roofing. A friend helped me with the furnace.

Danny and Davie

Family Diving

Dr. Nelson 'Doc' Mathison invited me to a meeting at his house, along with 'Big Jim' Christiansen, to set up a charter for his proposed diving club, the Long Beach Neptunes. The year was 1950. I am the only living charter member left.

Our club was very active and many wonderful weekends were spent at various places up and down the coast diving, with our families waiting ashore, for the makings of wonderful chowders, and barbecues that were prepared onsite by the non-divers.

Several club members came over to my house for a potluck get together with their wives and children. Along with my husband, Jake, and my first two sons, we decided to start a new club for families with children. The only prerequisite was that both mother and father had to be divers and have at least one child. We selected the name of Aqua Familias, meaning water families.

I had thee months to go before the birth of my third child, David. I was in the water every weekend until 10 days before the due date. It was another boy, so naturally another diver in the family. I was a nursing mother but refused to leave any of my family at home on our dive days with the club. We always took turns to go out diving, the men together and then the women got their time. When it came time for me to feed my son someone on the beach would wave a big white flag, which meant head for shore now.

Aqua Familias became very popular. By the time I had my fourth son, Daniel, two years later, we had had to close the club to any new members. We found a church basement in which to have our monthly meetings. During those years we were probably the most active skin diving club.

In My Own Words • Marriage and Kids

This Family Goes Diving for Its Dinner

By HERB SHANNON

It's a good thing everybody in the Frazier family at 266 Orizaba Ave. is crazy about sea food. Otherwise the government would have another surplus commodity problem on its hands.

Five of the six Fraziers are skin divers. Only Daniel, nine months old, has yet to don a face plate, and he's scheduled to start training in a couple of months.

Whenever the Fraziers trek down to the sea in rubber suits, which is two or three times a week, they come home with 50 to 100 pounds of abalone, scallops, crab, lobster, shark, octopus or other delicacies of the deep.

Some of the loot goes in the deep-freeze, some goes to relatives and friends, but mostly the Fraziers are their own best customers.

"We all like fish, shell or otherwise," explains Mrs. Dottie Frazier, speaking for her husband, Jake, a city fireman, and sons, Darrell, 14; Donald, 12; David, 3, and little Daniel.

"We save enough on food bills in a couple of weeks to pay for all our diving equipment," Mrs. Frazier adds.

Included in the equipment are swim fins, suits, face plates, spears and snorkel breathing tubes for the five active skin divers. The Fraziers also own a compressed air tank for extended living periods which they take turns using.

"We also have a skiff and outboard motor which we use for getting to the right locations," says Jake Frazier. "Both the older boys are expert swimmers and David floats around on an inner tube, but we expect him to start swimming this year."

The Fraziers swim the year around, preferring the winter "when the water is clear."

All this underwater activity started 15 years ago when Mrs. Frazier was given her first instruction by her father, former Harbor Commissioner Francis Reider.

Jake Frazier was inducted five years ago and became an addict when he came home the first day with a limit catch of abalone.

There are a few hazards to the sport, the Fraziers admit. All of them have suffered Moray eel bites, sea urchin stings and other minor injuries in combat with their prey.

But Mrs. Frazier, a certified skin diving instructor who has been helping the County Recreation Commission organize a water safety campaign, believes it is a sport eminently suitable for the average family.

"The only danger in skin diving is the lack of proper training," she maintains.

EXAMING part of one day's catch, the skin diving Frazier family anticipates a lobster dinner. From left, Darrell, 14; Mrs. Dottie Frazier; Daniel, nine months; Jake Frazier; David, 3; and Donald, 12.—(Staff Photo)

RESULTS OF THE LONG BEACH NEPTUNES contest in January. Left to Right—Bill Stack, Lee Jamison, Bob Washb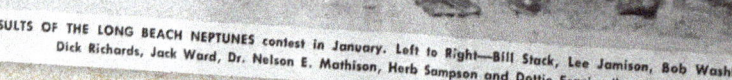Dick Richards, Jack Ward, Dr. Nelson E. Mathison, Herb Sampson and Dottie Frazier (kneeling).

Long Beach Neptunes
THIS CERTIFIES THAT
Dorothy Frazier
is a member in good standing of the L.B. Neptunes
19 53 to 19 54
D. M. Dottie
PRESIDENT

August 2019.
Dottie was honored at the Long Beach Neptunes club meeting as the last living Founding Member and presented with a Long Beach Neptunes throw. Shown on the right with the Riffe family.

66   *Trailblazer: The Extraordinary Life of Diving Pioneer Dottie Frazier*

Look... no hands!

In My Own Words • Marriage and Kids

My sons...
Darrell, Donald, David, and Danny

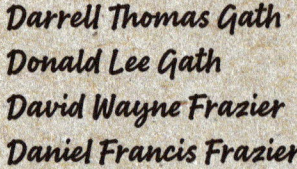

Darrell Thomas Gath
Donald Lee Gath
David Wayne Frazier
Daniel Francis Frazier

1964

1975

2004. Dave and Darrell with Dottie

1995. David, Danny and Darrell.

1995. Chance (Darrell's son), Darrell and Danny.

Trailblazer: The Extraordinary Life of Diving Pioneer Dottie Frazier

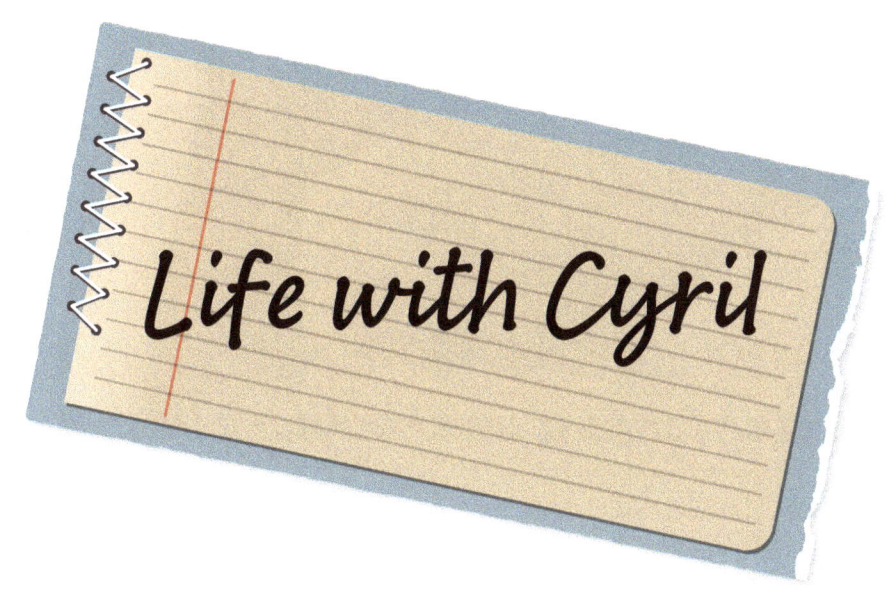

Looking for Surf and Finding a Husband

My fourth son, Daniel Frazier, had just turned 16 and was a surfer. He had recently taken first place in a surf meet and I had promised him a trip if he won AND if he brought his grades up to A and B. The race was on. As I anticipated, he came home with all Bs, and I was already half packed for the trip.

My Ford truck was in great condition: good tires, a stove, fridge, two bunks and a first-aid kit. There was lots of storage space for our skin-diving gear, hiking boots, fishing gear and my special tool kit, which I always take with me. Our surfboards and wax were always where we could quickly access them. And there was plenty of food for two always-hungry surfers. Our water tank was full, also the propane and gas tanks. We had sun hats, sunburn cream and sunglasses. I also brought my special fillet knives for preparing fish.

We were on our way by 4 am on the first day of school vacation. We crossed the border into Mexico, and after two long days of driving arrived at San Blas, Nayarit. Following directions from a tourist, we found Matanchin Bay. Within 15 minutes the boards were off the truck and we were paddling out to a nice-sized break. After an hour I returned to camp, ready for a good nap in the camper, but not before I thanked our guardian angel for our safe trip.

The weather, warm water, fishing and surfing were all A1. We spend most of the next week surfing; after all, that's what we came down for. We did take time off to gather lots of beautiful clams and fish for our meals. The estuary catfish were some of the best I had ever eaten. We were pretty well stocked for everything we needed, except for fresh milk.

There were six or eight other camper trucks parked close by, most of them containing surfers. They always

story short, we all stayed for another week. Cyril the surfer talked us into staying at a beach camp with hot showers, which sounded really good to me and Danny. We made trips into the jungle, caves where pirates were thought to have hidden their loot, and visited many interesting historical sites, which Cyril and I both enjoyed.

We invited Cyril to visit us in Long Beach on his way back to Canada, and he did, eventually making many trips to Long Beach. Cyril May and I were married in 1973.

It's an amazing miracle to find love where you never expected it. Who do I thank?

asked us if we needed anything when they went to the little pueblo six miles distant. They often brought us bolillos, delicious white sandwich rolls, from the bakery in town.

When it came time to head home, Danny wanted to take some bolillos with us. He had also been saving his money to buy certain white shirts that the boys at school favored. He wanted to take a dozen of the shirts home and sell them to his friends. We packed up and left the next morning for the pueblo first and then home.

We pulled into the central plaza and parked. There were many small shops and we priced shirts in all of them. About halfway through the shopping expedition Danny asked if I had noticed the man following us. I said I had, but commented that he just looked like a surfer. When we exited the last shop Danny went back to the fifth or six shop to make his purchase; coming out with his 12 shirts. He whispered to me that the guy was still following. I said I would ask the guy where the bakery is located, which I did. He responded with directions, saying he was going there as well and would be glad to show us.

It turns out that our bakery guide and his two friends were in San Blas on a surfing vacation and would be returning home to Canada in a few days. To make a long

In My Own Words • Life with Cyril

Oct. 1972. On our way to Mexico.

Our Days in San Blas

Editor's note: *The following is a letter Dottie wrote to friends back home in Long Beach, explain how she and Cyril spend their days in San Blas, a small fishing village in Nayarit, Mexico, The couple met in San Blas while each was on a surfing trip. They later married and built a home in San Blas, spending six months of each year there.*

When we receive mail here in Mexico, many of you ask what we do all day to keep from being bored. So I'm going to give you a sample of what we do over a period of a few days, to give you an idea.

We get up about 7 am after a sleepless night, thanks to the many biting insects that seem to ignore screen and bug sprays. After breakfast we load surfboards onto our motorbikes and ride the six miles to Matanchin Bay, a famous surf break noted for its long rides. If the surf is up, we surf for a couple of hours.

We both get some nice, long rides, and with only a few others surfing we have the place practically to ourselves. My only complaint about Matanchin is that I spend too much of my time chasing my board all the way back to the beach!

The beach stretches several miles, and at low tide vehicles can drive on the hard-packed surface. We put the boards back on the bikes and head for the center of the beach where we find a clam bed with cockles bigger than the ones we hunt at home. We gather clams and head back to the RV for a nice clam chowder. We are both more than ready for a good nap in the camper on the back of my Ford truck. The truck serves as our temporary home until the construction our future house is completed.

After supper we walk the quarter mile into town. We pick up some supplies, get our mail and check on the progress of our new home, which we do almost every day. We decide to attend a movie, which costs us 24 cents each. During the movie everyone talks, babies cry, scenes are missing everything goes black once or twice. For these reasons, we do not go to the movies very often. Back at the RV, we study Spanish for about an hour, a nightly task.

On another day after breakfast, we go down to the river and fish, catching five or six nice ones. I don't know what they are, but they taste good when they are cooked. If it runs, swims, flies or crawls I will hunt it and cook it.

Then we go swimming at our local beach right in front of our place. We soak up some sun, repair nicks in our surfboards, polish the bikes, and then it is time to fix supper. The moon is lovely, so we decided to walk down the beach and see our new home in the moonlight. We love it!

On another day we are again up at 7, then go over to our casa to plant trees. We put in three banana plants, one lemon tree and three papayas. We expect to put more in later. There are already two or three coconut palms with coconuts about ready to pick.

We play tourists today and explore an old fort up on the top of a hill. The year before I found two Boa Constrictors here. We are well covered with mosquito repellent and spend two hours exploring bat caves, hoping to find reptiles. I am almost clobbered by a big iguana that falls from the cliff above. It hits rocks several times on the way down, but scurries away after landing.

We are almost late for the big volleyball game at the school, Gringos vs. Locals. The score is 3-0 Gringos.

On another morning we launch our boat for the first time since we have been here. We head out fishing for the entire day. We catch a lot of fish, but the only one I recognize is Roosterfish. We release the fish that are not familiar to us. We cruise along the beautiful shoreline, enjoying the lovely weather and just being out on the ocean. Last year when we were here we explored as much as we could for diving, but the water is not very clear, the surf is rough and there are no nearby islands.

The water here just can't be beat for warmth and the surf is always good enough for body surfing or boards. Our new home is going up fast and it won't be long before we can move in. We can hardly wait and are never bored!

Love,
Dottie and Cyril

In My Own Words • Life with Cyril

Dredging for Gold

Cyril and I enjoyed taking off in our RV and finding places to try panning and dredging for gold. We found a place in Grass Valley where we could spend the night in the RV. In the morning we picked up a few supplies and headed up the mountains to the small town of Alleghany.

At the first bridge we came to we found a place to park the rig off the highway. We grabbed or gold pans and headed down a path to a nice stream. Suddenly, a uniformed policeman stepped out of the bushes and told us that we were trespassing on private property. We explained that we just wanted to try out our gold pans. He explained that all property along Kanaka Creek was guarded by armed officers and posted as private property.

He then added that he knew of a couple with a leased spots on the creek that might be able to help us. The couple had a small cabin and was dredging for gold on their leaseholds. The officers thought that we might be able to use some of the leaseholds, if we could find the couple.

After the officers gave us directions we took off in search of a dirt road a few miles on that turned down the hill to a creek at the bottom. With Cyril's careful driving, we made it. We found the cabin and saw a woman standing in the creek in water up to her waist. There was someone underwater next to her; we could see bubbles breaking the surface.

As we stood on the bank watching, the woman noticed us, then reached down and tapped the person in the water. He stood up immediately, demanding to know what we were doing there and asking what we wanted. Cyril explained about the policeman suggesting that we find and contact them to teach us about dredging. Cyril, with his Australian accent, broke the ice, and we were invited to stay and have lunch. The couple wanted to know all about Australia.

From that day and for many years to come, we were good friends with Bob and Donna, returning every summer to work on private property on any of their leases on the creek. We learned about using a four-inch dredge, sluice and air-compressor for underwater work. Wetsuits, weight belts, booties, gloves and hoods were needed to help protect us from the creek's frigid, snowmelt water.

We also operated a 2-inch dredge. Everything—diving gear and dredging gear—had to fit in our RV, and had to be carried down to the creek. We took turns working in the freezing water, operating the dredges to "vacuum" rocks off the bottom into the sluice above. We all helped each other, vacuuming back and forth, moving rocks.

During the time that Bob and Donna had been coming to Kanaka Creek from their home in Nebraska, the gold they found covered their expenses each summer and provided them with a wonderful vacation each year. When not dredging in the creek we saw deer, quail and several rattlesnakes. One evening sitting by our RV, a Black Bear came down the dirt road and started climbing up the hill above our camp. The bear did not seem interested in us. Another time, when Cyril was doing his daily jog up the road and back, a Mountain Lion crossed in front of him.

Diving with air pumped from a compressor was a great adventure. Small trout would swim right up to my mask and around my head, seemingly interested in what I was doing. After diving the four of us played cards. Cyril (a professional songwriter) and I entertained our hosts performing tunes written by Cyril. Cyril also played the guitar and we both played harmonica.

These were wonderful times that I will never forget.

1939

1941. Harley-Davidson circa '35 750 Flathead. Saddlebags loaded with abs and bugs from dive at Palos Verdes.

1951. Chuck Mikelson and Dottie on her Harley-Davidson.

1946

My Love Affair with Harleys

I have always loved Harley-Davidson motorcycles, and have been the proud owner of two of the legendary machines.

My affair with motorcycles began in the late 30s, when I belonged to a motorcycle club. On outings I was sometimes a passenger and sometimes the driver. I was usually the only woman at club outings.

A Harley entered my life in 1941 when a biking buddy was called up for military service, leaving his beloved 1935 Harley flathead in my care, until his return from duty. He told me if he didn't make it back that the bike was mine.

He never returned; a victim of the surprise attack on the *USS Arizona* at Pearl Harbor. I was still caring for and riding the bike and inherited it two years after his death.

Two years later I was left another Harley, this one with the knucklehead engine. I finally sold one of the Harleys, replacing it with a dirt bike. Three dirt bikes later I acquired a 185 Suzuki Enduro dirt bike, which I dearly loved for many years.

Epilogue: On February 19, 2019, Dottie sold her last motorcycle, a Kawasaki, to her doctor of 25 years, James Norcross, who purchased it for his son, Noah. Dottie decided to sell the bike after the DMV would no longer renew her motorcycle license. Her car license has been renewed until 2023.

Dottie with Noah (left) and Dr. James Norcross

From Dottie's first Harley Davidson in 1939 to her last Kawasaki in 2019, with many two wheelers in between, Dottie was never without a bike.

The Scuba Years

1957. Al Tillman and Dottie Frazier in "Intro to Scuba Diving."

1957. Darrell and Dottie between scenes for "Beyond The Reef."

Scuba Training

Returning from another Catalina weekend, 'Big Jim' Christiansen told me that he had just signed up for a scuba course to become an underwater instructor. Los Angeles County was offering the course. This was their fourth Underwater Instructors Certification Course (U.I.C.C.) and was to start in two weeks. Jim suggested that I join the course.

I told him that I had never tried scuba and didn't know the first thing about it. One of the first prerequisites, he said, was a thorough knowledge of skin diving, of which I was more than qualified. Second was a working knowledge of scuba, of which was a big zero for me. "I can teach you most of the bookwork in just the ride to and from class," said Jim, adding, "As for using the breathing apparatus, you can bluff your way through with me as your partner."

I was skeptical, but at his insistence I sent in my application along with my check to cover the cost of the course. On the day the class was to start, I received a letter from Los Angeles County thanking me for my interest, but they were sure that I would be happier taking a class at the local YMCA. I called Jim and told him that I had been rejected for the class. His first question was, "Did they return your check?" When I told him that they had not, he said, "Just be ready and I'm picking you up."

Arriving at the pool where the class was held, we were met by Al Tillman, the instructor, who immediately shook hands with Jim, telling him what a pleasure it was to have such a well-known diver join the class. Al then addressed me, "You must be Dottie Frazier, and didn't you receive my letter?" Jim spoke up, "Yes she did, but her check was not returned. Do you have her check?"

To this question the answer was "No, it's at the office." Then Jim said, "I guess she is a paid member of this class. Let's go sit down, Dottie."

There was considerable mumbling and grumbling from the other students (all males), and I felt more than a little uncomfortable. Jim told me to just ignore them.

At this point it is necessary to explain how foolish Jim and I looked as buddies for the class. Big Jim was 6 feet, 4 inches tall and weighed more than 200 pounds. I was barely 5 feet tall and weighed 110 pounds soaking wet. We ended up being called Mutt and Jeff, which was quite appropriate, given our appearance together!

I could not have bluffed my way through scuba gear if it hadn't been for Jim. He made me feel that I had always had the skill and knowledge. When I had to perform a simulated rescue with him as the victim I just about gave up trying to pull him to the other end of the pool. I still think that he used his fins a little and his arm underneath his body where it couldn't be seen, to assist me in completing this test. I'm glad it wasn't out in the ocean for real.

Our ocean checkout dive was on a sunless, cold and windy day with rough surf running. Two instructors had anchored inner tubes just past the surf line and visibility was poor. Each instructor took a team of two who swam out in full gear, checked in at the inner tube and were then told to dive to the bottom and proceed with a ditch and recovery. This exercise was one we had practiced in the pool, but the conditions far from ideal in the ocean. We had to sit on the bottom, take off our tank, weight belt and mask, which we tucked under the weight belt so it would still be there when we needed it. Jim was only a few feet from me, doing the exercise. We surfaced at the same time and so as not to lose our position.

We dove back down and immediately cleared our masks and sat down or I should say, I tried. Jim being so heavy didn't have any trouble but I was getting quite a buffering from the surge. Next thing I knew Jim got my attention and reached for the good-sized knife in his leg holster. He showed me how to stick it under a rock with the handle out at an angle and anchor my ankle under the handle. He handed me the knife and I followed his instructions. This allowed me to finish putting on my gear with out getting tossed around. Jim was a great teacher and a good diving buddy.

At graduation, Jim and I received the two highest grades, me for water work and Jim for written. We were also given seats on the board of directors for the Underwater Unit and staffed the next few classes.

That is how I became the first certified female diving instructor in the world. I went on to train more than 2,000 scuba divers.

D. Frazier, Scuba Instructor

I found a shop that was willing to take me on as their first scuba instructor, but only for a trial period. I made a sign announcing that a class would start soon: 12 students, first-come, first-served basis, instructor D. Frazier.

Because scuba was so new, no one signed up. For the next month I kept busy teaching skin diving and swimming lessons at the local YMCA. I spent every minute when not teaching learning how to make drysuits at the shop. The shop owner was also working on designs and patterns for a new type of exposure suit made out of neoprene rubber that was glued together. These were the first wetsuits and the first big order was from the Navy UDT (underwater demolition team) on Terminal Island.

I was so busy making drysuit and wetsuit patterns that I finally had to quit the YMCA classes I was teaching and concentrated instead on the diving suits. I had all but given up hope that a scuba class would become a reality. Then my boss told me one evening that a doctor had just signed up for a private class of eight, all medical men. The class would be held at a private pool at the residence of one of the men.

They would like the class to begin on the next weekend, four days away. Class would meet three days a week and on Saturday and Sunday.

Wow, my first class since I graduated from 4 U.I.C.C.! I was so excited that for the next four days I could hardly sleep at night. I had so many questions going through my head, including how could I teach diving medicine to a group of doctors? Worse, no one had mentioned that the instructor would be female. What would their reaction be when they found out? From the very first, diving was strictly a man's world, and it was almost unheard of for a woman to be a diver, let alone to become the first woman to become a scuba instructor.

It was Saturday morning, and my first scuba class would meet in the afternoon. I spent the morning giving a talk to a group of father and sons, dressing for the occasion in a very feminine cotton dress, high heels and silk stockings. There was no time after the talk to change into something more casual for the scuba class.

After I rang the doorbell at the address that I was given, the door was opened by a very nice-looking man who politely asked, "Well, what can I do for you, young lady?" I answered, "I am here to teach a scuba class." "Oh no, I'm sure there must be a big mistake. I'm sure the others in the class would agree that we wouldn't take lessons from a woman." I asked if I could speak to the others, and he agreed, so I followed him to the pool. I introduced myself, showed my teaching credentials and asked for a chance to talk to them before they dismissed me.

I explained that course would be divided into two sections, the first section being skin diving and the second section scuba diving. As part of the first section, tests would be given on swimming ability and the class would learn about skin-diving equipment and the marine environment.

"You will learn all about the use of swim fins, face plate, snorkel, rubber suits, weight belts, safety equipment and floats and be tested on each," I said. "You will learn valuable information about the marine life you will find in this area, including legal restrictions on sizes, seasons and limits on lobsters, abalone and fish. You will also learn about dangerous marine life, such as the sculpin, rays and eels. I will inform you of the first-aid treatment for any of the above."

I continued, telling them there would be a written test as well as tests using equipment in the pool. "I feel that I can teach all of you more than most other instructors can, as I was raised on a boat since I was six years old. I have been diving most of my life and have taught swimming and skin diving since my early teens.

"I would like the opportunity to teach at least the first half of the class, after which if you don't think that you have learned anything from me, I will see that you get all of your fees back and I will find another instructor to teach the rest of the class."

I left the room so the group could discuss the situation. I told them that I hoped I could be their instructor. Thirty minutes later I was given a unanimous affirmative from all.

Everyone passed the first section. I gave them a week to practice using their new skin-diving equipment and their new skills in the ocean. Each student reported their experiences to me.

Then we moved on to scuba. "This next section of our class will be all about Self Contained Underwater Breathing Apparatus, commonly referred to as scuba. You will learn about the regulator, tank, weight belt, atmospheric pressures in the water, diving diseases, buddy breathing, rescues, entry into the water from a boat and through the surf. This part will take 20 hours of class and pool work, after which there will be a 100-question written test. Then your boat dive at Catalina Island will finish the course."

One month later all members of the class passed and no one failed my very difficult written test. I was proud of my first class and of my new career as the first woman to become a scuba instructor in the world.

One of Dottie's first scuba classes, 1955.

Dottie's Firsts, Honors and Achievements

Born in 1922, as a young girl Dottie grows up within steps of the Pacific Ocean and is raised on boats by her father. Tomboy Dottie starts swimming at age three, rows a skiff at age five, sails competitively age six, uses a homemade diving mask (made by her father) at age six, and becomes an expert freediver and spearfisher by the time she is in her teens

1930s Dottie is known for her body surfing. She soon takes up board surfing, snow skiing, water skiing, competitive swimming, water polo and springboard diving

1940 Dottie starts teaching skin diving classes at the YMCA. She is also an avid hunter and motorcyclist

1942 Dottie graduates from the United Aircraft School as an aircraft mechanic, a 'Rosie the Riveter'

Mid-1940s Dottie works as a cook, deckhand, spotter and assistant helmsman on commercial fishing boats

1948 Dottie teaches swimming classes at the Big Pike Plunge in Long Beach

1950 Dottie become a charter member of the Long Beach Neptunes, the second oldest dive club in the U.S. Dottie starts another club, Aqua Familias. At weekend gatherings moms and dads take turn watching kids on the beach and diving

1950s Dottie is the first woman to commercially produce both drysuits and wetsuits. She begins manufacturing her own line, Penguin Suits, and make suits for U.S. Divers, Healthways and navy UDT teams

1950s Dottie is the first woman to own a dive shop, where she runs dive classes and sells her wetsuits

1951-1970 Dottie is an instructor for all Red Cross water safety programs, which include swimming, lifesaving, small craft, first aid and skin diving

1955 Dottie enrolls in the Los Angeles County Underwater Instructors Certification Course (4 U.I.C.C.), at the time considered to be too physically demanding for a female to participate. Dottie takes top honors in the class for water work, experiencing resentment from some of the other students (all males). She becomes the first woman certified scuba instructor in the world, overcoming prejudice to train more than 2,000 scuba divers.

1956 and **1957** Dottie is a coordinator and instructor with the Los Angeles County Underwater Unit.

1956 to 1963 Dottie serves on the board of directors for the Los Angeles County Underwater Unit

1956 Dottie trains as a hardhat diver. She works only briefly, finding the cumbersome gear to be too uncomfortable and restrictive on her petite frame.

1960s Dottie acts in films that feature diving, including *Beyond the Reef*, circa 1961, and *Introduction to Skin Diving* with Al Tilman

1993 The Academy of Marine Sciences & Underwater Research chooses Dottie for inclusion in *Who's Who in Scuba Diving*

2000 Dottie is inducted into the Women Divers Hall of Fame

2000 Dottie is honored as a "Mother" of the sport by freedivelist

2001 Dottie is honored as a Life Member of the second oldest dive club in the U.S., the Long Beach Neptunes. She is the only surviving charter member

2009 Dottie is an International Legends of Diving honoree, the only woman that year

2011-12, Dottie is a multiple medal winner in billiards and racquetball at the National Senior Games

2013 Dottie is honored at the Amazing Women Awards, Lifetime Achievement, sponsored by the *Long Beach Press-Telegram*

2014 Dottie is honored as Senior of the Year, Long Beach City College

2014 Dottie is honored with the California Scuba Service Award for her contributions to the California sport diving community.

2017, at the age of 95, Dottie goes on a YMCA camp zipline flight and loves it so much that she goes right back for a second flight. She plans to repeat the feat for her 97th birthday

2019 Dottie is awarded the Historical Diving Society Diving Pioneer Award. She is the only fourth woman to be honored, following female diving notables Dr. Eugenie Clark (2015), Dr. Sylvia Earle (2007), and Lotte (and Hans) Hass (1997).

Dottie is the only female diver honored by inclusion in the Museum of Skin Diving History

Nitrogen Narcosis

A trip to Catalina Island was planned to relax and enjoy doing just nothing. I had just finished a scuba class of young men who had been hard to teach. I thought they would never absorb the materials or complete the water work necessary for graduation. I had to work with them many extra hours. Finally, I was convinced that they were knowledgeable enough not to drown. I then issued certification cards to each of them.

A long-time diving buddy invited me for the weekend aboard his 22-foot cabin cruiser. I hoped that I could enjoy some much-needed relaxation. We had a good crossing and dropped the anchor at Parsons Landing, one of my favorite Cove's on the West End of the island. Visibility was crystal clear, so we decided to dive straight away. We jumped in with just our mask, fins and snorkel, making a leisurely swim around the area to enjoy the beauty of the submarine gardens that Catalina is so famous for. We hunted limits of lobster and abalone, then went back onboard to work on our tan and snooze.

After a light lunch we decided to get our scuba gear on and head to Ship Rock, just out of the Isthmus, where the water is much deeper, and see what we could find out there. We decided we only had enough time to use up one tank before we had to head for the mainland, before the wind came up. We anchored, suited up and headed down. We checked out some nice caves and crevices for big bull lobsters. I had stopped about halfway to the bottom to look under some enticing rock ledges. When I finally backed out my buddy was nowhere in sight.

I decided to swim a circle to look for the telltale bubbles coming up from his regulator, which would indicate where he was. I was in the last of the circle pattern when I finally found bubbles. I followed them down to the bottom. I had expected him to wait until I had exited the ledge. Instead, he had descended about 40 feet deeper. When I found him, he was standing on the bottom with his mouthpiece hanging by his side. I swam up in front of him, grabbed the mouthpiece, and tried to get him to put it back in his mouth. He was fighting to keep me away. I managed to get him to take a couple of breaths, but he took the regulator out of his mouth again. When I tried the second time he struck me in the face, knocking my mask off. If he had hit me that hard on the surface, I'm sure he would have knocked me out, but underwater the blow was just an inconvenience. I found my mask, put it on and cleared the water out.

It suddenly occurred to me that my buddy was suffering from an attack of nitrogen narcosis, a diving disease that I had first heard about in my instructor's course. I had never talked to anyone who had experienced it or been witness to an attack. It occurs at depths usually greater than 60 to 80 feet, and symptoms vary with different people. I had been too occupied to see how deep we were. My only concern was how I was going to get the mouthpiece back into his mouth and start him towards the surface, forcing him to exhale slowly as we ascended. If he held his breath he would surely get an air embolism, which could prove fatal without immediate medical attention and a decompression chamber close by.

I got around in back of him, grabbed his mouthpiece and held it over his mouth with one hand while releasing his weight belt with the other hand and letting it drop. This gave us positive buoyancy and we started to rise slowly. I reached around his tank and across his chest pulling inward as hard as I could to force him to exhale. By this time he was keeping his mouthpiece in and breathing through it. He started relaxing after we ascended about 30 feet off the bottom. By the time we reach 30 feet from the surface, he gave me the OK sign, stopped struggling and was exhaling on his own the rest of the way up.

We got back onboard the boat and stowed our gear. I then asked him if he remembered anything that had just occurred. He said that when he left me he was chasing a big Sheepshead fish that was headed straight for the bottom. He was totally amazed at the different fish of all sizes that were all around him and so friendly! He decided then that he did not need that thing in his mouth and that he could breathe just like the fish were doing. It was at that minute that I showed up. If I had not got the air to him who knows how this story might have ended.

All's well that ends well.

86   Trailblazer: The Extraordinary Life of Diving Pioneer Dottie Frazier

My Big Lobster

My 18-year-old son Darrell graduated from the Los Angeles County Underwater Instructors Course, 8 U.I.C.C., in 1959. I believe he was the youngest male to graduate, and we were the only mother-and-son team that I had heard of. To celebrate, we were making a dive at the Long Beach breakwater. We had just finished our tanks of air and had a good supply of scallops, eight legal lobsters between us, and a few Black Abalone. I used them to make pickles, as the local abalones were not as good to eat as the ones from the islands.

Since I still had some air left I decided to go down and check for a couple more bugs. I must have been feeling lucky, because the first big crevice I looked in I could not believe what I saw. It was the biggest lobster I had ever seen. It was quite a ways back in the rocks, but I started easing slowly back and so far, he hadn't moved. I knew I was out of air and I had better get out of my gear right away and head up to the boat where Darrell could get my gear aboard.

I rested for a few minutes after delivering my gear, then hyperventilated a few breaths, then dove back down to the big bug hole. Being small, I was able to slide in easily to where I could see his antennae moving slightly. I reached with my left hand above his head, wiggling my fingers to keep him looking at them. I did likewise with my other hand, reaching up and over his head. Now he was within reach.

I made a fast grab at his right feeler and at the same time I grabbed with my left hand at his horn, connecting with both at the same time and getting a pretty good grip on the lobster. I started backing out by using my knees, my elbows, legs and any other part of my body, all the while hugging the unbelievably huge crustacean to my stomach. I prayed that I could get it to the surface before I blacked out from the need of a breath of air.

It was just pure luck that I made it out of the rocks and up to my boat, where my son was waiting to help me hoist it in. He said he had worried about me being down so long and was just about ready to head down to see if I needed assistance.

There is only one picture of that lobster, taken by a friend when we got back ashore. Darrell and I did not have a camera with us on the dive to the bug hole.

Trailblazer: The Extraordinary Life of Diving Pioneer Dottie Frazier

Editor's note: Dottie wrote The following poem after diving with Lynn and Keith Chase on their boat, Sea Chase. On page 103, Keith writes about sharing adventures with Dottie in his story, **A Feisty Gal**.

Aboard the *Sea Chase*

By Dottie Frazier

September first, nineteen seventy-five at six o'clock,
Met Keith and Lynn on the *Sea Chase* at the dock.
Said goodbye to Cyril and stowed my gear away,
Untied all our shore lines and headed out of the bay.

The *Sea Chase*, built sturdy and a nice smooth ride,
An experienced skipper with his wife by his side.
The Chases both sacked out and I took over the wheel,
Escorted out by seagulls and one old Harbor Seal.

From Long Beach to Oxnard, about a six-hour run,
For a three-day adventure and looking for fun.
Four divers onboard and at home on the ocean,
So none of us expect to be worried by motion.

I throttled back once, which shook the Chases a mite,
To release a bird that had misjudged his flight.
It crashed on deck but his wings were okay,
So we helped him get airborne without delay.

At Channel Island Marina we fueled up the boat,
Took a tour of the harbor then tied up to a float.
The harbormaster assigned us to Slip J 29,
Later, snug in our berths, we opened up some wine.

We all went ashore for a much-needed walk,
Then back to the boat for eats, drinks and talk.
In the A.M. at seven we took another aboard,
Don Salveson proceeded to get his gear stored.

Our ETA was figured to the time we'd arrive,
So I set the compass course for two eighty five.
T'was an overcast day but a sea calm and nice,
I counted thirty-four sharks and big sunfish twice.

No stormy weather made us all smile,
So our crossing was perfect to Santa Cruz Isle.
We arrived in good shape but a hungry bunch,
And while fighting off yellowjackets we ate our lunch.

One left it's stinger in my upper left arm,
And so to say the least it caused me alarm.
In beautiful Fry's Cove we dropped our hook,
Donned our dive gear to go in for a look.

I forgot my vest so was uncomfortably cold,
But for the diving here I am really sold.
Got scallops and bugs and nice legal abs,
Speared good-eating fish but didn't see crabs.

Went on shore for a hike by a nice little stream,
Green ferns and flowers, it wasn't a dream.
Sheep on the hillside and pretty, small trees,
Lots of birds and those darn yellow bees.

A relaxing evening with music and song,
Great seafood dinner to last the night long.
Next morning we rose feeling spry as can be,
Headed up the coast on a cold choppy sea.

Found some protection in a snug little bay,
Dropped both anchors so the boat would stay.
Excited to have a new spot to explore,
Overanxious divers, always wanting to see more.

Never get bored and see wondrous things,
Colorful fish swimming by as if they had wings.
Sometimes a shark or an eel in a cave,
But nothing to fear, they really behave.

Another good place we heard was nearby,
So before it got dark we'd go give it a try.
Supposed to be hot springs near to the beach,
In Little Lady's Canyon, so not out of reach.

In the afternoon Lynn and I took a hike,
Looking for that place that we'd both really like.
So it wasn't too long before we were both taking a bath,
Hoping no one else would come up the path.

Lying in a warm pool with the sun shining bright,
Gazing down to the ocean, the *Sea Chase* in sight.
Not a worry or care, our minds all at rest,
Just enjoying the day, a blessing at best.

No news from the mainland for this period of time,
So didn't have to hear of politics or crime.
Hated to get out, it felt especially great,
Please, a few minutes more, dinner can wait.

Back to our temporary home on the sea,
To supper, card games and a tired, happy me.
We hated to leave but commitments we had,
We depart in the morning so all of us sad.

One more dive we decided, before heading to port.
We all agreed diving was our favorite sport.
So to Fry's we went since it had been number one,
And finished our diving that had been so much fun.

It was an easy job when we arrived at the float,
With four of us working to clean up the boat.
These days of fun in the month of September,
Being with good friends I'll always remember.

Thanks Lynn and Keith for a wonderful time.
This brings to the end my short story rhyme.

    Lovingly,
    Dottie Frazier
    September 1, 1975

Face to Face with a Great White

In the 1960s I was busy making exposure suits in my dive shop, Penguin, when I got a phone call from a diving buddy. "Get your gear together and in two hours we will pick you up at the airport where Jack has his plane. We're going to Mexico for a two-week trip." My oldest son Darrell could run the shop for me while I'm away, as he had done in the past. It took me about 30 minutes to get my diving gear into my backpack, along with a few personal items that I would need. I met the plane as scheduled and we took off for Mexicali. We got all of the necessary credentials stamped, filed a flight plan and off we went.

Our first stop down the Baja Peninsula was Bahia de Los Angeles, on the Sea of Cortez. One of our group had heard about this place and had made previous arrangements for four of us with diving included as well as all meals. When we finally arrived over the small village, which had a very rough, small landing strip, we saw burros on the runway. We buzzed the runway numerous times to scare them off, with no success. By this time the people in the village who were expecting us sent a man out. He was riding a burro and swinging a large palm frond from one side to the other, chasing burros off the runway so we could land.

It was only a short walk from the plane to the little house belonging to Papa Diaz, who was to be our host for the next week. It consisted of a small cooking area, a bare room with a long table and stools for at least 10 or 12 people. There was an adjacent open room with cots, and the roof was made of palm fronds. There was an outhouse about 50 feet in back of the house. Out in the open near the beach was a makeshift shower. The only bath available was in the warm waters of the Sea of Cortez.

Our first meal was made up of beans, tortillas and hunks of meat that we were told was turtle, but when the truth was known at dinners end, turned out to be burro.

We found the burro to be on the tough side but edible. Mama and Papa Diaz and their two little sons were at our table every meal and spoke no English. Between the four of us we managed the language barrier, with some additional help from a Spanish/English dictionary.

Señor Diaz owned the only sizable and seaworthy boat in the village large enough to accommodate seven or eight divers and their gear. It was called a panga, a modest-size, outboard-powered open fishing boat popular in Mexico. There were many small islands not more than a couple miles offshore. We were told that there were lobster, scallops, oysters and many different kinds of edible fish in large quantities. We spent several enjoyable hours diving. Our catches helped feed local families.

We usually went diving in the early morning as the wind came up in the afternoons. During off time we explored the mines and the hills within walking distance. One morning we headed out in the panga to Smith Island, the largest one around. We were told that game fish were plentiful there. We went to the north side of the island where our guide anchored the panga. I was startled at what he was using for an anchor; about 10 pounds rusty cable wrapped around several large, homemade hooks. The hooks snagged rocks on the bottom to keep the boat in one place.

All four of us jumped in and headed out in different directions. It was a beautiful warm day with water temperatures in the 80s. I had already speared some nice fish, which I had put in my bag and headed back to the boat. It was no wonder, that after 2 1/2 hours in the water I was getting a little bit tired and my legs felt like they were about ready to cramp.

It was then that I heard some yelling and looked up towards the boat to see everybody was already aboard and waiting for me. They were standing up and waving their arms and yelling, "Dottie, there's a shark coming up behind you!" I looked behind me and saw a huge fin about 100 feet away. I remembered reading about what to do around sharks: don't make any splashes, drop beneath the surface, and keep facing the animal as it circles.

I kept submerging, moving closer to the boat and watching the circling shark. I got within about 15 feet of the boat and felt my calves starting to cramp. I had already dropped my game bag the minute I saw the shark. The water was crystal clear and I could see that Jack and the guide were at the bow, trying to haul up the anchor, but it seemed to be stuck on the bottom. I surfaced, and heard Doc yelled at me to wait till the shark was in the circle heading away from me, then swim and kick towards the boat. However, the shark didn't make a full circle; it suddenly turned and headed straight for me.

I didn't know what to do and figured I was already a meal for the shark. When the shark moved towards me I turned and swam as hard as I could towards it. I imagine it was wondering what was this thing coming at it. The shark hesitated and then shot off to the side, which gave me a chance to swim straight to the boat. When I got closer I held my arms straight out and up and Doc and Jack lifted me to safety. I cried like a baby and couldn't stop shaking for quite a while.

My diving buddies in the boat and watched the entire scenario, but thought it foolhardy to dive in and help me and just be more food for the shark. Doc said, "I hope you don't pull that stunt again, Dottie, because the next time you start swimming towards his mouth he's going to open it bigger and you're going to swim right on in!"

The shark was huge and the guide kept saying, "Tiburón Blanco Grande." I guess it meant Great White Shark. To me, it looked like a big submarine with a mouth.

We waited about 30 minutes before the boys were game enough to jump in and free the anchor. I had nightmares for a long time, reliving my close call with a Great White.

Editor's note: none of the photos shown here were taken that day.

In My Own Words • The Scuba Years

Training and Life Accomplishments

Compiled by Dottie Frazier

- Horseback riding
  - Exercise girl for quarter horses
  - Rode my palomino in rodeos and parades
- Sewing
  - Made my own clothes
- Cooking
  - Worked in restaurants
- Boating
  - Owned and skippered sail and powerboats
- Commercial fishing
  - Deck hand
  - Galley girl/cook
  - Served as crew in sailboat races
- Sculling
- Canoeing
- Kayaking
- Swimming
  - Pacer for channel swimmers
  - Competitive swimmer
  - Water ballet
  - Water polo
  - Junior Olympics long distance swimmer
- Camping
- Backpacking
- Hiking
- Scouting
  - First Girl Scout in Long Beach
  - Counselor for Girl Scout camps
  - Scout den mother for 10 years
- Instructor
  - Water safety, lifesaving, swimming, sailing, small craft, canoe, kayak, power boats, first aid
- Skiing
  - Team acrobatic water skiing
  - Water skiing shows
  - Snow skiing
- Surfing
  - Body surfing
  - Short and longboard surfing
- Tennis
- Raquetball
- Volleyball
- Billiiards (Snooker and pool competitions)
- High Diving
- Music
  - Violin, Accordion, Ukulele, Harmonica, Piano
  - Singer
- Waitress
- Bartender
- Secretary
- Bookkeeper
- Model/actress
- Gardener
  - Raise most of the fruits and vegetables I eat
- Lifeguard
- Gun expert and hunter
- Diving manufacturer plant foreman
- Dive shop owner/manager
- Wetsuit designer and manufacturer
- Scuba regulator repair
- Retail sales
- Skin and scuba diving instructor
- Qualified hardhat diver
- Chauffeur
- Taxi driver (car and boat)
- Schooling
  - Brown's and Flintridge private schools
  - Graduate of Long Beach Polytechnic High School
  - Attended Long Beach City College for many years
  - Aircraft repair school graduate
  - Graduate of 4 U.I.C.C. (Los Angeles County Underwater Instructors Certification Course), 1955
- Property owner/manager for more than 79 years with working knowledge of:
  - Maintenance, painting, wall papering, stucco work, carpentry, hanging doors and windows, damage repair, screen repair, furniture refinishing, plumbing and electrical
- Handicrafts
- Fresh and saltwater fishing
- Ranching
  - Milking and butchering
  - Raised rabbits and chickens for eating and for shows
- Expat, lived in Mexico for 10 years (six months at a time)
- World traveler
- Boarding house owner/operator
- Home baker
- Raised four sons
- Public speaker
- Volunteer at a children's clinic
- Volunteer during World War II at Mare Island Navy Hospital
- Milked rattlesnakes for antivenom for hospitals
- Philanthropist

Let The Games Begin!
Three Gold Medals in raquetball, 1965-1969
Five Gold Medals in billiards, 2011 - 2014

Dottie's 9 ft pool table with ball return and fast cloth

Laguna Woods Pool Club

2006. My 84th birthday and still playing racketball with my dear friend, Zoe for more than 20 years!

City College Racketball 1981

Many years of modeling ... above and below water.

U.S. Divers catalog 1962

Voit Mfg. Co.

Bel Aqua drysuits

Singles magazine

Outdoor News Magazine

waterski suits

Body Glove

Long Beach City College 2014
"Learning Lasts a Lifetime" Award

International Legends of Diving 2009

Press-Telegram Amazing Women 2013 Lifetime Achievement Award

Hunting has been a part of my life since I was a little girl. My dad and I hunted together in desert areas throughout California and Arizona, mostly for rabbit, quail and ducks. As an adult, my annual hunting trips were as important to me as my spearfishing, helping me to feed my family and my boarders.

Dottie's backyard garden in Long Beach includes pineapples, grapes, squash, rhubarb, beets, tomatoes, artichokes, beans, plums, apples, eggplant, onions, brussel sprouts, figs, strawberries, cucumbers, turnips...
and, she eats everything she grows!

Dottie Frazier and her Women Divers Hall of Fame sea sisters... at the Long Beach Scuba Show celebrating Dottie receiving the 2014 California Scuba Service Award and "pre-Catalina Hyperbaric Chamber Night" get togethers in Dottie's backyard...

2013

Chamber Night at the Long Beach Aquarium of the Pacific, 2011

2014

99

Lynn Chase with Dottie at the Monterey Bay Aquarium

A Feisty Gal

By Keith Chase

Lynn and I used to see a lot of Dottie when we lived in Southern California. One summer Dottie hosted Lynn's daughters on her boat at the Isthmus at Catalina Island. The girls still recall all the fun they had with Dottie. They got in lots of freediving for abs and Dottie prepared some delicious seafood meals.

When we got together we always enjoyed Dottie retelling some of her more hair-raising tales of adventure. We sometimes would see each other at the Isthmus and she would also tell stories about the goings on at Doug's Bar, where she worked.

We once enjoyed a weekend together with Dottie on our boat, *Sea Chase*, at Catalina. By then she had sold her boat and was just happy to be back at the island to visit old haunts and friends, and, of course, to get a little diving in as well.

We had a grand time that weekend enjoying a full raft of Dottie stories. She told us about her many trips to Baja and her fish camp. She loved those trips to Baja.

Another thing she loves is her Harley. Last time we saw her she said the DMV would not renew her license to drive her bike. They renewed her car driver's license, but not the bike. They must have thought that she would be a menace to others on the road!

Anyway, Dottie is a dear friend and she has remained an important influence during our years of being a part of the diving community.

Keith and Lynn met at a Long Beach Neptune's holiday party in 1965. Lynn was a Los Angeles County underwater instructor, graduating in 1962 with 11 U.I.C.C. Keith and Lynn soon became diving buddies. Keith was involved in the early days of the Under Water Photographic Society. Both Keith and Lynn assisted with the Santa Monica Film Festival. Lynn and Keith were married on April 20, 1968, right after Keith graduated from 17 U.I.C.C. The couple taught basic scuba classes together for several years.

Around 1970 they purchased *Sea Chase* and spent the next 20 years exploring the California coast and Channel Islands. They also traveled extensively to international diving locations.

Lynn worked as a superintendent for recreation and retired from the City of Carlsbad in 1990. Keith worked 33 years for a multinational chemical company. They are members of the Los Angeles Yacht Club and Keith is past president of both the Underwater Photographic Society and the Adventurers' Club of Los Angeles.

The couple moved to Carmel in 1995. They volunteered as docents at the Monterey Bay Aquarium for 17 years. The couple lives at a retirement community in Pacific Grove where Lynn receives full-time care for Parkinson's Disease. The Chases have been married 51 years.

Dottie, Keith Chase and Barb Allen, 2016

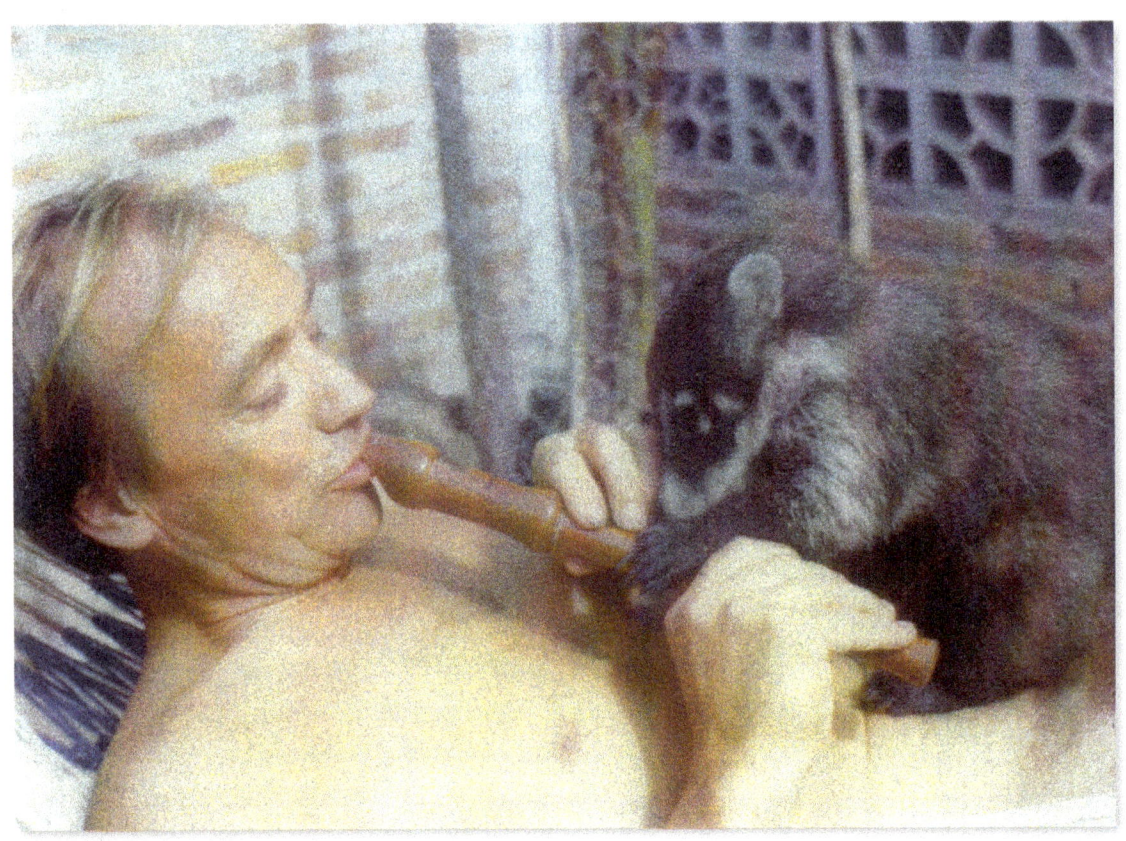

Happiness is a Coatimundi

By Cyril May

"Honey, there's a coatimundi!" These words were uttered by my wife, Dottie Frazier May, as we walked through the outdoor market in San Blas, Nayarit, Mexico, a tropical paradise where we were blessed to live six months of the year. I looked and saw a man leading a young coatimundi, about two months old, on a leash, just like he was out walking a dog.

A coatimundi, also known as coati, are members of the raccoon family and native to South America and Mexico. At first sight they are often confused with possums, raccoons, bears and even monkeys. They walk on all fours, although can stand on their hind legs, like a bear. The hindquarters are larger than the front legs, resulting in the animals walking with a forward sloping stance. The nose is ludicrously long and almost prehensile, as is the tail. The monkey-like fingers and toes are long with strong, curved claws for catching and holding everything from small fish and crabs to spiders, beetles, fruits and nuts.

We asked if the animal was for sale. After some bargaining we found ourselves the owner of a coatimundi, which we promptly named Katrina. We soon learned more about coatimundi characteristics, namely that they are bundles of boundless energy AND mischievous rascals on four legs.

We carried Katrina to our motorcycle, looking doubtfully at each other. "Dottie, I think you had better hold her between us," I said, straddling the bike. Dottie climbed on, tightening her grip on Katrina's collar. I kicked the bike over and it started with a roar. Katrina's immediate response was a stream of excrement. We drove the short distance home, mustering what little remaining dignity we had.

Not sure what she might do, we decided to leave her

on a leash and settled her in the shower stall with a box of rags for a bed. She soon became a loyal member of the household, running freely about the house and grounds with our two dogs. This is not to say there was not any trouble. Jars crashed down and pots clanged onto the floors as Katrina's insatiable curiosity led her to explore everything in the house. We finally moved things to safer spots and rearranged as best we could our more valuable items.

"Why that little ____," came Dottie's voice from the bedroom one day. "What's she done now?" I yelled back from the kitchen. "Just come and see what the little devil has done. Look at this mess," Dottie said, "the whole roll of toilet paper!" I looked from one bedroom to the other and back to the bathroom. Katrina had done an excellent job, better than any cat could have managed. Toilet paper was everywhere, entwined around legs of beds and bureaus in random profusion.

The first time we took Katrina fishing with us on our 12-foot boat kept us on our toes every minute. Nothing was safe from her curiosity. She reached out to touch sharp hooks and lures and got tangled in our lines. Finally, we landed a fish, a seven-pound yellowtail. It flapped around our legs in the bottom of the boat, Katrina attached to the back of the fish, like a cowboy on a bucking bronco. We finally got Katrina off the fish, the lure out of pant leg and the fish in the bag.

On one quiet morning, Dottie was preparing hotcakes for breakfast. I was taking down a picture from the hallway when a big gecko fell from behind the picture onto the floor. I called for Katrina to come catch the gecko, one of her favorite pastimes. She came at a run, causing the gecko to take off at high speed toward the kitchen, Katrina in hot pursuit.

At this point one of our dogs showed up to see what was going on. Gecko and coatimundi slid between the startled dog's legs, unable to stop their forward momentum on the tile floor. The dog, in panic, leapt backwards, colliding with Dottie who was just lifting flapjacks off the stovetop. The hotcakes hit the floor, the dog hit the hotcakes, the gecko made it safely under the stove, Katrina smacked into the stove, and Dottie burned her arm on the hot pan. "Sometimes," said Dottie, "I just don't know about that coatimundi. Just imagine when she's fully grown, she'll be a disaster going somewhere to happen." I had to concur.

Epilogue

When Katrina reached about eight months of age and our six-month visas were close to expiration, the question arouse, what about Katrina? A decision had to be made. U.S. Customs would never allow her to enter California and it wouldn't be fair to leave her behind to be kept in a cage. We were also concerned about freeing her near our fishing village as coatimundi are sometimes eaten as a delicacy.

After careful deliberation, we put Katrina on the seat between us and took off on the Suzuki. Down rough dirt roads, sand trails, through thick, lush jungle to a beautiful cove on the edge of an estuary. We climbed off the bike and put Katrina on the ground. A loud commotion in a tall coconut palm overhead caught our attention. Looking up we saw a beautiful, fully grown male coatimundi. He climbed down, unafraid. He headed straight for Katrina. A few nuzzles and grunts from the male and she was in love. Only a glance back over her should at each of us as she followed him into the jungle.

We felt a great loss at that moment and fought back the tears that were welling in our eyes, hoping we had done the right thing. We like to assume that they had a good, safe life together, and were blessed with lots of little ones.

Katrina had filled six months our lives with a love and affection that we will always cherish and never forget.

Cyril May was born in 1929 and raised on a farm in Victoria, Australia. As a young man he left Australia to work his way through the South Sea Islands and Canada. In the early 1970s May's surfboard washed him onto the beaches of San Blas, Nayarit, Mexico. He finally settled down in Long Beach, California with his American wife, Dorothy "Dottie" Reider Gath Frazier May.

May's philosophy of life is reflected in the words and music he has been writing for more than 40 years. May's lyrics tell of his personal search for gold, feeling the freedom of hang gliding, the purr of his motorcycle on the open road and his never ending love of Australia.

His music, in collaboration with Jack McDonald, has been recorded on three albums, and a hit song was used for a movie and a television show. Dottie contributes harmony on many of May's songs.

Adventure is her Middle Name

By Eric Hanauer

Editor's note: Adapted from Diving Pioneers, An Oral History of Diving in America, by Eric Hanauer. Dottie was 72 at the time of the interview.

When I interviewed Dottie for *Diving Pioneers,* she told me becoming an instructor was easy compared to selling the diving public on being taught by a woman.

"I walked into Penguin Dive Shop in Long Beach and asked, 'Do you have an instructor?' They said no. I said, 'How about giving me a try?' 'No, if we're going to, we're going to have a guy.' I said, 'Well at least give me a chance. You don't have to tell them I'm a woman. Just say D. Frazier is your instructor. If they don't like it, you don't have to pay me.'

A private class for doctors was a success, and Dottie's career as a scuba instructor flourished.

"Penguin was a complete retail dive shop owned by Lyle Anderson, who also had a beautiful pool out in Park Estates," recalls Dottie. "He had a 40-foot cabin cruiser which I used for all the Catalina dives. We would stay over at his home in Avalon, dive Saturday and Sunday. A good setup."

Eventually, Dottie bought the shop from Anderson. She made custom wetsuits and set up a network of 48 dealers throughout the United States. "I made the suits for UDT in Terminal Island, Honolulu and San Francisco. I tailored every suit myself, gave a 100% guarantee as long as I took the measurements. Our suits were just glued, I never sewed a suit, and we had about five assemblers.

"My son, Darrell Gath, also an L.A. County scuba instructor, managed the shop when I was out playing. I worked seven days a week, teaching every night or doing ocean dives, for about 18 years.

"I got out of the business when they started sewing everything...the machines were really expensive. I'd never had a zipper come out or had a suit come apart. Then I got very sick, and sold out because of illness around 1970. I later worked for Healthways, was the only woman foreman they ever had. I also designed a suit for U.S. Divers and for Healthways, based on my Penguin models."

After selling the dive shop Dottie continued managing her father's hotels, apartments and flats. "I do all the plumbing, hiring gardeners, hanging doors and minor painting," she states.

Dottie has been diving in Australia, Japan, New Zealand, Hawaii, Canada, the Caribbean, Mexico and Italy. "I have all my gear, but I don't scuba much any more. It's too hard to haul tanks around, and my equipment is so antiquated.

"I'm 72 now, and think about the 80s coming up. I think I still hold the record for being the oldest female racquetballer at City College. Right now I'm playing at least three to four days a week at the YMCA, all with guys. I still ride a motorcycle, water ski, backpack and skin dive.

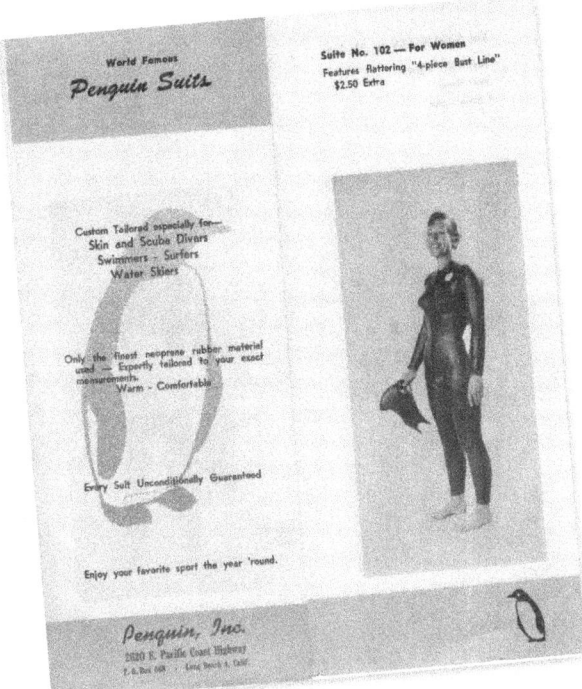

Penguin Dive Shop, Long Beach

"Now maybe I'll have time to enjoy my four sons and get to know some of their offsprings, teaching them how to enjoy all the sports I still love.

"There's no age limit," says Dottie. "I don't want to quit for a while."

Eric Hanauer has been diving for more than 60 years. He has been published for more than 40 years as a writer/photographer in diving publications worldwide. As a scuba instructor he certified 2,000 students at the university level. He is the author of four books on subjects ranging from travel to history.

For the first 16 years of Eric's career diving took a backseat to swimming. He was a successful swimming coach at the high school and university level, and developed the grab start, now used by competitive swimmers everywhere.

Eric founded the scuba program at Cal State Fullerton, and for 35 years was its Diving Safety Officer and a founding member of AAUS (American Academy of Underwater Sciences). He developed classes in basic scuba, free diving, advanced scuba and underwater photography.

His first magazine article appeared in *Skin Diver* in 1977. That launched a second career as a writer and photographer that took Eric around the world in the heyday of the magazine industry. He wrote an oral history series for *Discover Diving*, which eventually led to a book, *Diving Pioneers*.

Eric was married for 20 years to Mia Tegner, a marine biologist at Scripps Institution of Oceanography. Before her death in a diving accident in 2001, they collaborated on many projects, including a Red Sea guidebook, and many science-based magazine articles.

Since 2004 Eric has been married to Karen Straus. Like Mia, she is a member of the Women Divers Hall of Fame, and collaborates on many projects. Along with Bonnie Toth, they recently co-authored a coffee table book commemorating the 75th anniversary of the invention of the Aqua-Lung. Commissioned by Aqua Lung, it was translated into German, Italian, and French editions.

Eric Hanuer and Karen Straus in Dottie's backyard.

Dottie and security guard with a couple of crabs for dinner!

Women Divers Hall of Fame sea sisters Dottie, Barb and Drey Stockert

Barb and Dottie at the 2014 Long Beach Scuba Show where Dottie received the California Scuba Service Award.

Diving with Dottie

By Barbara Allen

In 1957, Dottie was the only female scuba instructor during my 6 U.I.C.C. instructor certification course with Los Angeles County. I was the second woman certified as a scuba instructor; Dottie was the first.

We became friends and she used to visit me when I lived at 'The Ranch' in Sorrento Valley, San Diego. The house was on a few acres and the valley ran all the way to Torrey Pines Beach. There were no neighbors or developments in the valley back then.

I recall on one occasion that I was still at work when Dottie arrived at The Ranch. She decided to go adventuring to a nearby stream/slough area. When I came home that night frog legs were on the table for dinner! On another occasion Dottie prepared rabbit. Dottie was the best guest to have; she loved to cook and always left the house better than when she arrived.

I had many memorable trips with Dottie in the 1960s at the Isthmus, Catalina Island. She worked ashore and lived aboard the *Fickle Miss*, her 21-foot boat with twin outboards.

One of the most memorable trips was heading to the Isthmus via Avalon one weekend. Suddenly her boat stopped dead just outside the mooring buoys. The Harbor Patrol comes right out to offer a tow, but Dottie says "Heck no, if I can't fix it I don't belong out here." She grabs her toolbox, finds and fixes the problem and we're off again!

One fun night dive at the Isthmus was with Ron Church and Bob Bradley, co-pilots of Westinghouse's Deepstar submersibles. We (mostly Dottie!) out dove the guys for bugs.

In 1969 Dottie and I headed to Glover's Reef, 28 miles offshore of Belize, for some pristine diving and underwater photography. We overnighted in New Orleans, treating ourselves to beignets at Café du Monde. The next morning we flew into Belize City, staying a couple days with Canadian friends who then joined us for a couple days at Glover's.

On the way out to Glover's our boat stopped at a couple islands to deliver supplies. It was the off-season and we were the only guests at the resort. The diving was superb. Dottie hunted for fresh fish and turtle for our dinners.

Barbara Allen grew up in Los Angeles with active, athletic parents who introduced her to camping, fishing, swimming and body surfing. While teaching swimming, paddleboard ballet and lifeguarding at the Los Angeles Swim Stadium.

Barbara graduated from L.A. County's 6 U.I.C.C. in 1957, the second woman after Dottie Frazier. After graduating from Los Angeles City College she worked for SoCal Gas and taught scuba for the Meistrell brothers at Dive 'N Surf.

She moved to San Diego to work at General Atomic and taught scuba for the Diving Locker and at General Atomic for its recreation club. In 1961 Barbara became the secretary of the fledgling San Diego Underwater Photographic Society.

In the mid-60s Westinghouse established an ocean research laboratory (WORL) in San Diego and Barbara was hired as a technician.

In the early 70s Barbara moved to the Bay Area and worked for FMC's oceanographic and waste treatment divisions. She then worked for Bechtel San Francisco.

In the early 80s Barbara returned to Bechtel for a two-year assignment in Pennsylvania. Back in San Diego in 1986 she took off for a year-long drive around Australia. Back in San Diego Barb started traveling in Baja again and took a job with the City of Carlsbad, retiring in 2012.

In April of 2009 Barbara was honored as a Pioneer by the San Diego Underwater Photo Society. In 2014 she was inducted into the Women Divers Hall of Fame.

1969

Jenna Frazier, Dottie's granddaughter

My Firecracker Grandma

By Jenna Frazier

When you're out having drinks with friends, there usually isn't much discussion about each other's grandmothers. That is, of course, unless you are the grandchild of Dottie Frazier.

Even without knowing Dottie, you can't help but love her. And if you have had the pleasure of meeting her, you know she can put a smile on anyone's face and is arguably the most fascinating woman in any room.

Growing up with Dottie was humbling. The woman has accomplished so much in her ninth decade of life. Just this morning, I received an invite to attend a banquet, honoring her with yet another pioneer award for diving. And a pioneer she is. First female scuba instructor, an early hard-hat diver, first female dive shop owner, first female wetsuit designer, and the list goes on.

As a child, visiting my grandma would leave me feeling inspired. These visits would start with a tour of her garden, sampling the fresh berries, vegetables and the sweetest passion fruit you've ever tasted. Next came a game of billiards. You'd think as a 10-year-old kid she would have some mercy on you. Well, if you know Dottie and her competitive nature, you'd know you were wrong. Even now, she's willing to take the money of any unsuspecting visitor who thinks they're going to hustle this 5-foot tall, 97-year-old firecracker at a game of pool.

Next, we'd sit around and listen to stories told of diving trips past. A born storyteller she is, and I could sit and listen to her for hours on end in perfect contentment. If you walk around her home, there are diving artifacts that relate to the stories. All throughout her house and yard are underwater relics displayed on shelves, fences, and hung on her walls, each with a story to accompany it.

Looking back, I truly believe that these stories I had been hearing for the last 20-plus years are what inspired my love for travel. In 2013 I was off to Thailand and knew that I had to see what this diving thing was all about. A group of friends and myself stumbled upon a diving resort in Koh Tao and, by the end of the day, we had signed up for a 5-day PADI course.

Day one, found me up early after a night on the town, sunburned to a crisp from the day prior, and undoubtedly questioning my decision. However, after a few hours of instruction, we were off to our first real dive. Jumping off the boat came with a lot of apprehension, but as we made our descent and the nerves calmed, I looked around.

At last, I understood why this fearless woman was so fascinated by and humbled by the sea. I couldn't help but feel her with me as I took in all of the beauty around me and, looking back, although she wasn't there with me, to this day it stands as one of my fondest memories of her.

Since that summer, my dive logs entries have been scarce. I entered graduate school and have spent the past years inundated with my studies. However, as I gain more free time, I look forward to dives to come and to gaining a deeper appreciation of the sport Dottie holds so dear to her heart.

I can't help but feel an overwhelming sense of pride to think that my grandma has had such an impact on the sport that has had such an influence on her life.

Jenna Frazier is the granddaughter of Dottie Frazier. She grew up surfing and fishing with her father and sister and her love for water continues to this day. Jenna completed her undergraduate studies at San Diego State University before continuing on to graduate school at Western University of Health Sciences, where she obtained a master's degree in Physician Assistant Studies. She now lives in San Francisco with her partner and works as a physician assistant specializing in orthopedic surgery. Jenna enjoys traveling the world, hiking, camping, and spending time with family and friends.

Dottie next to her life size cutout at the Huntington Beach Surf Museum, 2002

Acknowledgments

The Riffe family with Dottie

I would like to thank my family and my many friends who have helped to make my life so adventurous. Life is a precious gift, and I am grateful to have had the opportunity to share it with you. I apologize in advance for any inadvertent omissions.

My sons, Darrell Thomas Gath (deceased), police officer; Donald Lee Gath, aircraft industry; David Wayne Frazier, police officer; and Daniel Francis Frazier, fire department captain

A partial listing of my grandchildren and great-grandchildren and their spouses, Debra Ellingson and her husband, Mike; Dennis Gath and his wife, Cindy; Jenna Frazier, Nicole Buczynski and her husband Sean; David Frazier Jr. and his wife Tiffany; Jeffrey Gath, Drew Brown, Don Gath Jr., and Danelle Mehler

Cisco Ayala

My friends Tom M. Mellor, Andrea Stockert, Cisco Ayala and his wife Patty; Heidi Nye, Kathrene Doerschuk, Sonia Diaz, Dr. James Norcross, Robbie and Brenda Elroyd, Betty Koehler, Julie Riffe, Sam and Betty Miller, Fredy Koorey, Barbara Allen, Sue Baker, Clare and Chuck Codora, Jim Steffens, Lito Rangel, Danny Echeto, Bob Keller, Joi Hanley, Alfredo Velascos, Patrick Stearns, Lora Lee Meistrell, Dorothy Cherney, Julie D'Angelo, Karma Lodoe, S. Stephen Sollitt, DDS and Choeun Anna Chem

My financial managers, Mike and Danna Myers

Tom Mellor

A California native and scuba diver since 1978, Bonnie Toth is creative director and owner of Bonnie Toth Advertising & Design in San Clemente, CA. For more than 35 years, she has shared her passion and creativity elevating the marketing world through outstanding visual communications and advancing exploration of the undersea world through her deep commitment to diving and leadership in the industry. Bonnie served on the Board of Directors of the Women Divers Hall of Fame for 14 year and is currently the Graphics and Website Coordinator. Bonnie is the Managing Editor for *The Journal of Diving History* and was the designer of Aqua Lung's coffee table book, *Immersion: 75 Years of Adventure and Discovery.*

Bonnie was inducted into the Women Divers Hall of Fame in 2007. In 2014, she received the Historical Diving Society E.R. Cross Award for Distinguished Service and the BTS Diver of the Year for Distinguished Service. Bonnie also received the prestigious Academy of Underwater Arts & Sciences NOGI for Distinguished Service in 2016.

Karen Straus was born in Southern California and grew up in Nairobi, Kenya. She started diving in 1968 after taking a scuba certification course in college. She was among the first handful of women certified as scuba instructors, earning her Los Angeles County instructor certification in 1970. For many years she taught swimming, life-saving, and skin and scuba diving in Orange County, California. She also began writing about and photographing marine life for dive magazines and books. She spent the next 20 years in Montana, Maine, Chicago and New York working as a newspaper reporter and photographer, a food writer and editor, and a writer and field producer for underwater and nature television programming. Karen is a long-time officer of the San Diego Underwater Film Exhibition. She was inducted into the Women Divers Hall of Fame in 2011. In 2017 she was the co-author of *Immersion: 75 Years of Adventure and Discovery,* about the invention of the Aqua Lung regulator. In 2018 she was a contributor to *Ocean Metaphor, Unexpected Life Lessons From the Ocean.* She is a contributing editor to *Dive Training* magazine.

Book cover photo editing / retouching: Erin Quigley

www.ingramcontent.com/pod-product-compliance
Lightning Source LLC
Chambersburg PA
CBHW061749290426
44108CB00028B/2937